THE BODHISATTVA'S EMBRACE

Dispatches from Engaged Buddhism's Front Lines

ALAN SENAUKE

CLEAR VIEW PRESS | BERKELEY

Portions of this book have previously appeared in different forms in: *A Buddhist Response to the Climate Emergency, Adbusters, Buddhadharma, Jewish Voice for Peace, Religion East & West, Turning Wheel, Umbrella Man — Recollections of Sojun Mel Weitsman by His Dharma Heirs.*

Published by Clear View Press
1933 Russell Street
Berkeley, CA 94703
www.clearviewproject.org

Library of Congress Cataloguing-in-Publication Data
Senauke, Alan.
The Bodhisattva's Embrace: Dispatches from
Engaged Buddhism's Front Lines / Alan Senauke.
p. 243 cm. 13.335 × 20.32
ISBN 978-0-9827844-0-2
1. Engaged Buddhism. 2. Zen Buddhism. 3. Human Rights —
Asia. 4. Race & Civil Rights — United States.

Cover photograph by Alan Senauke.

Back cover photograph by Peter Cunningham

TABLE OF CONTENTS

<u>APPENDICES</u>

PHOTOGRAPHS & GRAPHICS

Cover: at Dr. Cynthia's Mae Tao Clinic, Mae Sot, Thailand — February 2000

To My World: poem by Alan Senauke, illustration & design Nancy Werner — San Francisco, 1970

1. Two girls: Mae La Po Hta, Burma — February 2000
2. B.R. Ambedkar diorama: Ambedkar Museum — Nagpur, India — 2010
3. A.T. Ariyaratne (Sulak Sivaraksa in background): Sri Lanka — 1999
4. Robert Aitken: Hawaii — 2001
5. Novice Monk: Shwedagon Pagoda — Rangoon, Burma — December 2007
6. Police Van: Rangoon, Burma: December 2007
7. Exiled Saffron Revolution Monks: Mae Sot, Thailand — December 2007
8. Dalit Children: Kondhanpur, India — March 2010
9. Students at Nagarjuna Training Institute: Nagpur, India — March 2010
10. Broken Ships: Chittagong, Bangladesh — 2000
11. Mohammed, young worker: Chittagong, Bangladesh — 2000
12. Shipbreaking Workers: Chittagong, Bangladesh — 2000
13. Notes to God: Western Wall, Jerusalem — 2001
14. The Real Thing — Pune, India — March 2010
15. Columbia University Campus — April 2008
16. San Quentin Prison: California — 2010
17. Sojun Mel Weitsman Roshi: Berkeley Zen Center — 2006

Photographs by Alan Senauke
Back Cover Photograph by Peter Cunningham

TO MY WORLD

MINE IS LIKE BROKEN

BOTTLENECKS

AS YOU ARE DIZZIFIED

IN YOURS

THE TRUTH IS

WE ARE ABOUT AS TOUGH

AS WINDOWS

FRAGILE BUT YEARNING

TOUGH ENOUGH

ON BOTH SIDES

TO GO WIDE OPEN

ALAN SENAUKE

INTRODUCTION

The Bodhisattva's Embrace is a collection of personal essays on engaged Buddhism, or perhaps more accurately, the experiences and views of an engaged Buddhist. Some pieces are descriptive, some prescriptive, some more (or less) Buddhistic, and some provocative.

It is hard to define engaged Buddhism. But I think it has to do with a willingness to see how deeply people suffer; to understand how we have fashioned whole systems of suffering out of gender, race, caste, class, ability, and so on; and to know that interdependently and individually we co-create this suffering. Looking around we plainly see a world at war, a planet in peril.

Some days, I call this engaged Buddhism; on other days I think it is just plain Buddhism — walking the Bodhisattva path, embracing the suffering of beings by taking responsibility for them. In almost every religious tradition there are similar ways and practices integrating faith and activism. Across religions and nations we are each others' sisters and brothers and allies. Our effort is to be more truly human.

The first step on the Buddha's Eightfold Path is Right View. This means at once seeing what is right in front of us, and seeing to the bottom of things. It was the same in Shakyamuni Buddha's time. In an early Pali sutra, a seeker inquires:

> The inner tangle and the outer tangle —
> This generation is entangled in a tangle.
> And so I ask Gotama this question:

Who succeeds in disentangling this tangle?

The Buddha responds: "It is the wise person, established in virtue, having cultivated consciousness and understanding who can disentangle this tangle." Even if I fall short, I'll keep working at that tangle. If you want to sit down next to me, I welcome your help.

Coming back to Right View, I would add that each step on the Eightfold Path includes and implies the other seven. In that sense, Right View is Wisdom manifest. Right View is, as Shunryu Suzuki Roshi said, simply seeing "things as it is."

Wisdom is inseparable from Compassion, the active principle. This brings to mind the "Three Tenets" as developed by Bernie Glassman for the Zen Peacemaker Circle.

> Not-knowing, giving up fixed ideas about ourselves and the universe.
> Bearing witness to the joy and suffering of the world.
> Loving actions towards ourselves and others.

Not-knowing means approaching people, community, and society without fixed ideas or belief systems. It reminds me of Suzuki Roshi's epigraph to *Zen Mind, Beginner's Mind*: "In the beginner's mind there are many possibilities, but in the expert's there are few."

Bearing witness marks the subtle and often rapid shift from perception to conceptualization to action. In the space of Buddhist practice, mindfulness intervenes one step ahead of reactivity and habit. Having come fresh to a new reality, we begin to form ideas, compare them with our experience, and share these ideas with others. The tradition of bearing witness has two intertwining implications. First, it means to see what is right there for us to see. Second, it means to testify, to carry our witness to other people and places.

This naturally leads to loving action, compassionate action. Witness calls forth responsibility. That responsibility is to ourselves, and to all other beings — who comprise the vast reality I call my <u>self</u>. The circle of engaged Buddhism is unbroken.

I began to work as Buddhist Peace Fellowship's executive director in the winter of 1991. I had been practicing Zen for some years and was starting out as a priest. I was also the new father of a daughter, who is now a young woman, and then a son. My activist background went back to the early 1960s, first in a suburban civil rights group outside New York City, then in the student movement of the late 60s, moving on to radical anti-imperialism in the 70s. In the stormy and despairing late days of the Vietnam War I lost faith in nonviolence as a way to transform society. I was in the wilderness for a time, and it took almost a decade to find my way home again.

Coming to BPF, and continuing today with my own Clear View Project, I have renewed faith in nonviolence as a matter of training and discipline. I believe there is a way to be in the world that combines social transformation and principles of practice.

The Bodhisattva's Embrace is my attempt not to define engaged Buddhism but to speak of it from the inside: inside the practice itself, inside the conditions of life itself — with its joys and sorrows — at home and around the world. The bodhisattva vow is my watchword, the prime directive: Sentient beings are numberless; I vow to save them.

How to save sentient beings? The devil is in the details. A friend of mine cited his teacher, the late Kobun Chino Roshi. Chino Roshi, who died not many years ago trying to save his five-year-old daughter from drowning, once told his students: "Compassion is the activity of walking <u>with</u> another side by side. Not too fast, not too slow...same speed." And it is the activity of embracing, dancing with each other. Merging.

Again, in bodhisattva practice, wisdom complements compassion. Distinct words, inseparable practice. The essence of Buddhist wisdom is impermanence. As Suzuki Roshi said: "not always so." Compassion includes the reality that circumstances change, as do our thoughts about circumstances. This applies to individual lives as well as to the conditions of nations and societies at large. Things are always incomplete, unfixed.

The 13th century Zen master Eihei Dogen wrote: "When dharma does not fill your whole body and mind, you think it is already sufficient. When dharma fills your body and mind, you understand that something is missing." If I worry about what is missing, then I suffer. If I accept that "something is missing," then I am free to allow causes and conditions to change. With enough skill maybe I can help others do the same.

This book's structure is loose, but I have tried to create an overall shape and sequence. The first pieces delineate teachings and practices of engaged Buddhism and Zen from my point of view. As you can see from the title essay, "The Bodhisattva's Embrace," I lean heavily on what I have gleaned from Zen practice and wisdom. I often come back to the teachings of Dogen Zenji, who writes, "To study the Buddha Way is to study the self." I believe one begins to heal the world by looking at oneself, closely, inwardly. With this root of practice one can then begin to see how society itself is shaped by the forces that shape each of us.

I have been an internationalist as long as I can remember, personally and politically. Over the last twenty years I have been privileged — the right word, a double-edged sword — to travel and bear witness to wars, civil strife, poverty, and also to practice and liberation. Although my home is the Zen school, I have always felt that, as Marley's Ghost proclaims, "Mankind was my business. The common welfare was my business..." So the sequence moves to a series of essays on international experiences and analysis. I hope that, in places, I have conveyed some little of what I have been given to see and taste and touch.

Coming back home, I look at the workings of race, privilege, violence, and redemption in the United States. There is no way to step outside of one's skin. Dogen says, "If a fish leaves the water, it will die at once." Neither can we leave the ocean of society we inhabit. But can we live in a way that values, honors, and does not exploit those around us?

The last piece, "Things Fall Apart," honors my teacher. It also returns to basic Buddhism and the endless unfolding of impermanence. Is this suffering or liberation? It is within one's own power, and no one else's, to determine this. I hope to be there with you in the work.

I have also included a number of my photographs here. My hope is that they inform and reinforce the words, images making distant people and places more real.

THANK YOU

Along the way many people have helped me with my thinking and writing, and with their friendship and teaching: Robert Aitken, Melody Ermachild Chavis, Peter Cunningham, Mangesh Dahiwale, Samdech Preah Maha Ghosananda, Bernie Glassman, Paula Green, Tova Green, Ruben Habito, Shodo Harada Roshi, Annette Herskovits, Margaret Howe, Jill Jameson, Stephanie Kaza, Ouyporn Khuankaew, Ken Kraft, Anchalee Kurutach, Taigen Leighton, Diana Lion, David Loy, Joanna Macy, Zenju Earthlyn Manuel, Jarvis Masters, Susan Moon, Thich Nhat Hanh, Shohaku Okumura, Donald Rothberg, Maylie Scott, Jon Sholle, Sulak Sivaraksa, Vidyananda Soon, Kaz Tanhashi, Santikaro Upsaka, Phra Paisal Visalo, Jonathan Watts, Diana Winston, Lewis Woods, and many more, known and unknown. Thanks to Alex Kantner for proofreading, to Maria Winston for entering corrections and to Laurie Senauke, Ken Knabb, and Sandy Rothman for copyediting.

My children, Silvie and Alexander, do their best to keep me honest, with minds that are sharp and open, and with hearts that embrace the world.

Day to day, year after year, two people have helped me find my true life. They encourage me; they point to the path when I stray. I owe them everything: my root teacher Sojun Mel Weitsman, and my wife and partner Laurie Schley Senauke.

July 2010 — Berkeley, California

TWO GIRLS: MAE LA PO HTA, BURMA — FEBRUARY 2000

THE BODHISATTVA'S EMBRACE

(Note: The full translated text of Dogen's "Bodaisatta Shishobo"/"The Bodhisattva's Four Embracing Dharmas" can be found in Appendix 1.)

1. INTRODUCTION

To embrace is to encircle. I wrap my arms around you; you put your arms around me. To embrace is to unify, to make one of two. An act of love. In embrace, the limits of body, skin, feelings, and thoughts are all transcended. Seen at a distance, two beings are one.

There is a legend in Asia that Bodhisattvas practice deep in the forests, saving our world from destruction. They enact interdependence by embracing the world, beyond good and bad. These Bodhisattvas are quiet engines of salvation humming along beneath the surface of our societies and our selves. Maybe they even have a special dance

Bodhisattvas are spiritual masters who live with a vow to save all sentient beings. The word "Bodhisattva" means "enlightened being" or "enlightening being." Ancient Jataka tales tell about the previous Bodhisattva lives of Śākyamuni Buddha. A prince offered his own body to feed a hungry tigress. A parrot put out a forest fire by endlessly shaking river water from his wings. A hare sacrificed himself to make a meal for a beggar who was actually Śākra, king of the gods, in disguise.

In "Bodaisatta Shishobo," (The Bodhisattva's Four Embracing Dharmas) Dogen writes, "In the human world, the Tathāgata took the form of a human being. From this we know that he did the same in other realms."

Even today there are countless Bodhisattvas, taking just the right form to lead us to liberation. Taigen Leighton writes of these Bodhisattvas as psychological archetypes. This is true, of course. Each of us, no matter how deluded, has qualities of mind, character, and action that can benefit others. Instead of saying "Ladies and gentlemen," Zen teacher Nyogen Senzaki, who brought his "floating zendo" from Japan to California in the early twentieth century, used to greet his Western audiences as "Bodhisattvas." His greeting was an embrace, and a gentle way of prodding his Zen friends to see their deepest qualities.

The great spirits are more than archetypes. They are real people. They walk and talk and practice Dharma with their bodies. Martin Luther King Jr. or Mother Theresa or the Cambodian monk Maha Ghosananda are Bodhisattva models for us because of what they did in the world, because they persevered in the face of violence, discouragement, and countless dark nights of the soul. When we meet such beings, whether or not we understand or agree with them, we feel embraced, and instinctively we respond.

A Bodhisattva's vow to save all sentient beings means that she chooses to live within the world of karma, or cause and effect. A Bodhisattva embraces even failure with a willingness to begin again and again.

Buddhism is a universal religion. Its core truth is that each of us is continuously expressing Buddha-nature. This very mind and body is Buddha. You and I are Buddha. No one is outside the circle of awakening. We are Buddhas manifesting as Buddhas. And, although every being is Buddha, we are still in need of cultivation. Shunryu Suzuki Roshi said, "Each of you is perfect the way you are...and you can use a little improvement." This improvement is cultivation. It consists of practices that each of us must take on, not for self-improvement, but for the sake of peace. The *Vimalakīrti Sutra*, one of Mahayana Buddhism's key texts, describes the Bodhisattva's social mandate for peacemaking in terms of manifesting and cultivating.

> During the short eons of swords,
> They meditate on love,
> Introducing to nonviolence
> Hundreds of millions of living beings.
>
> In the middle of great battles
> They remain impartial to both sides;
> For bodhisattvas of great strength
> Delight in reconciliation of conflict.
>
> In order to help the living beings,
> They voluntarily descend into
> The hells which are attached
> To all the inconceivable Buddha-fields.

In "Bodaisatta Shishobo" ("The Bodhisattva's Four Embracing Dharmas") Dogen Zenji offers four specific and interlocking tools and practices for cultivating and manifesting as Bodhisattvas in the midst of society beyond the temple's walls. And when we use the proper tool to help others — following Avalokiteśvara, who in each of her thousand hands wields a tool for liberating beings — we become free.

2. DOGEN ZENJI AND THE **SHOBOGENZO**

Dogen Zenji brought the traditions of Soto Zen from China in the early part of the thirteenth century. He is a towering figure in the history of Japanese Buddhism. Dogen's birth is shrouded in mystery, but we do know that in the year 1200 he was born into an aristocratic Kyoto family. His parents died when he was still a child. It is said that, at the age of eight, smoke rising from incense at his mother's funeral impressed upon him the sad and inescapable reality of impermanence. At thirteen Dogen became a monk at Mount Hiei, the great monastic center of Tendai Buddhism in Japan. Practicing meditation and devotion day after day, he sought an answer to a question that fueled his great doubt.

> Both exoteric and esoteric teachings explain that a person in essence has true Dharma-nature and is originally a body of "Buddha-nature." If so, why do all Buddhas in the past, present, and future arouse the wish for and seek enlightenment?

If we are already Buddhas — if we are already saved and inherently awake — why do we need to practice? Actually, this is a central issue in every faith tradition.

Dogen's Tendai teachers suggested that an answer might be more readily found in the Zen school, which didn't flinch at ambiguity. Dogen took up his investigation with Master Eisai, a monk who had studied Rinzai-style Zen in China, bringing it to Japan for the first time in 1191. Eisai died in 1215, and Dogen continued his studies with Eisai's successor Myozen, who became Dogen's close friend and mentor.

Together Myozen and Dogen made the perilous journey to China in 1223, visiting the Zen monasteries of Southern China. Myozen settled down at one of these training centers, but Dogen continued to look for his true teacher. In 1225 Myozen passed away. In the same year Dogen found his teacher Rujing at Mount Tiantong. Rujing and Dogen recognized each other immediately, and Rujing gave this young disciple permission to come to his room with questions at any time of day or night.

One evening during the summer training period, Rujing shouted at a sleepy monk, "When you study under a master, you must drop body and mind. What is the use of single-minded intense sleeping?" Dogen, who had been sitting next to the chastened monk, suddenly experienced a great awakening. All his previous doubts were resolved. He went to Rujing's quarters and offered incense. Rujing asked, "What is the incense burning for?" Dogen replied, "My body and mind have dropped away. That is why I come." Rujing verified this experience and formally transmitted the Dharma to Dogen. Dogen returned to Japan as a Zen master. He later wrote:

> Not having visited too many Zen monasteries, but having only studied under my Late Master Rujing, I plainly realized that the eyes are horizontal and the nose vertical. Without being deceived by anyone, I came home empty-handed.

But he did come home with clear ideas about Buddhism rooted in *zazen*, the meditation practice he described as "practice-enlightenment." Against the usual notion of meditating in order to attain realization, Dogen proposed that the practice of *zazen* is itself the expression of realization. He stood conventional Zen on its head. Yet he was clear one still had to take up a rigorous practice of self-study in order to see the truth that is always right before our eyes.

So Dogen set up temples and monasteries, with rules based on his Chinese experience, and he began to write about Zen practice from every imaginable angle. *Shobogenzo* (*Treasury of the True Dharma Eye*), his masterwork, was begun in 1233 and its writing continued for fifteen years. As a religious and philosophical work, it is perhaps unmatched in any culture for the depth and challenge of its ideas, and for the difficult beauty of Dogen's language. Dogen is one of those rare writers who uses words themselves to go beneath and beyond the conceptual trap of words. We can see this in "Bodaisatta Shishobo" (The Bodhisattva's Four Embracing Dharmas), which became Chapter Twenty-Eight of the *Shobogenzo.* "Bodaisatta Shishobo" was written in the summer of 1243, shortly before Dogen's community abruptly left Kyoto for the remote mountain forests of Echizen. Historians are not certain why this move was so sudden, but there is a strong suggestion of sectarian conflict and possibly violence between Dogen's community and other more established sects. Perhaps it was the urgency of conflict that turned Dogen's thoughts in the direction of these Bodhisattva practices.

3. THE BODHISATTVA'S FOUR EMBRACING DHARMAS

Shishobo or the Four Embracing Dharmas are Giving, or *dāna;* Loving-Speech; Beneficial-Action; and what Dogen calls Identity-Action. Each dharma or practice is a method for connecting — a way to manifest the truth that we are not separate from each other. Because we are truly not separate from others, these four Dharmas allow Bodhisattvas and sentient beings to become free from the poisons of greed, hatred, and delusion. In embrace there is no distinction between self and other, between a Bodhisattva and an ordinary being.

These were already ancient practices in Dogen's time. They are found as the four *sangaha vatthu*, the Foundations for Social Unity in early Pali texts like the *Sangaha Sutta*: *dāna*, generosity; *piyavaca*, kindly speech; *atthacariya*, helpful action; and *samanattata*, cooperation or impartiality. In the Mahayana tradition, they appear in the *Lotus Sutra, Māhaprajnāpāramitā Sutra*, the *Vimalakīrti Sutra* and many other well-known teachings.

GIVING
The Bodhisattva's essential practice of peace is giving. Giving one's attention, friendship, and material aid. Giving spiritual teachings, community, and organization. Giving fearlessness. Giving is the first *pāramitā* or perfection, and it includes all other perfections. Dogen begins "Bodaisatta Shishobo" by explaining that:

> Giving or Offering means not being greedy.
> Not to be greedy means not to covet. Not to
> covet commonly means not to flatter. Even
> if we rule the four continents, in order to of-
> fer teachings of the true Way we must simply
> and unfailingly not be greedy. It is like offering
> treasures we are about to discard to those we
> do not know. We give flowers blooming on the
> distant mountains to the Tathāgata, and offer
> treasures accumulated in past lives to living
> beings. Whether our gifts are Dharma or mate-
> rial objects, each gift is truly endowed with the
> virtue of offering, or *dāna*.

Giving begins with oneself. I give myself to practice, and practice offers itself to me. In my search for peace, I find there is
always the pervasive smell of war. The taste of tears, corrosive
doubt, and decay fall within the circle of my own body and
mind. A war goes on here, right where I hide behind a mask
of self-attachment. If I hide out in a shelter of privilege, I cut
myself off from others. True giving is receiving the gift of *zazen*
mind and passing it to others in words and deeds. It means not
hiding. It also means giving fearlessness by showing others
that I am willing to face conflict, my own failure, and despair
as a natural part of being completely alive.

We offer gifts and guidance in many forms. At the heart of
these teachings is the understanding that peace is making connection. On a basic level, material goods are given. On a higher
level, teaching is shared. And on the highest level, there is just
connection, the endless society of being, the vast assembly of
Bodhisattvas. In his wonderful book *The Gift*, Lewis Hyde describes dinner in a cheap restaurant in the south of France.

> The patrons sit at a long communal table, and
> each finds before his plate a modest bottle of
> wine. Before the meal begins, a man will pour

his wine not into his own glass but into his neighbor's. And his neighbor will return the gesture, filling the first man's empty glass. In an economic sense nothing has happened. No one has any more wine than he did to begin with. But society has appeared where there was none before.

The gift itself is only a gift so long as it remains in circulation. A monk or nun carries an empty bowl from house to house. The bowl is emptiness, yet in this material world, food is offered so that one may live. Emptiness and form embrace and dance. Having eaten, the monk or nun transforms food into action and practice, which is offered to nourish all beings. The dance of peace continues. Again from Lewis Hyde:

> I would like to speak of gratitude as a labor undertaken by the soul to effect the transformation after a gift has been received. Between the time a gift comes to us and the time we pass it along, we suffer gratitude. Moreover, with gifts that are agents of change, it is only when the gift has worked in us, only when we come up to its level, as it were, that we can give it away again. Passing the gift along is the act of gratitude that finishes the labor.

Giving is not an abstract thing. It takes place in the world itself. Dogen writes:

> To provide a boat or build a bridge is offering as the practice of *dāna-pāramitā*. When we carefully learn the meaning of giving, both receiving our body and giving up our body are offering. Earning our livelihood and managing our business are, from the outset, nothing other

than giving. Trusting flowers to the wind, and trusting birds to the season may also be the meritorious action of dāna.

In all our worldly actions, we should consider what others need and what we can give them without nourishing our own self-centeredness. This is always a difficult practice. Dogen says bluntly, "The mind of a sentient being is difficult to change." Amen to that! This is true for others, and even more for ourselves.

LOVING-SPEECH

Loving or kind speech means telling the truth in a way that leads to right action. The Buddha suggested that before speaking we consider whether our words are true, useful, and timely. All three characteristics have to be present. Will my words actually be heard? And will they have a good effect?

Words are like arrows, or heat-seeking missiles. Once spoken they head straight for their target and cannot be called back. They have a capacity to wound or to heal, so their use calls for great care. Dogen writes:

> Loving-Speech means, first of all, to arouse compassionate mind when meeting with living beings, and to offer caring and loving words. In general, we should not use any violent or harmful words.

Two books by the late Zen teacher Dainin Katagiri were edited from his talks. The first book was titled *Returning to Silence*. This is the silence of *zazen*, the vast and still ground of being, which is spoken about in the mystic teachings of every tradition. His second book was *You Have to Say Something*. I don't know whether this pairing was the editors' conscious intention, but it represents something basic about a life of Buddhist practice. After his enlightenment under the Bodhi tree,

Śākyamuni Buddha was intending to remain in blissful silence. But the gods Brahma and Indra begged him to teach, to say something, and so he did. He taught us how to be intimate with the silence in all things. Silence informs all we are and all we do. For the sake of all beings, we have to come forth from that silence into the world of words and actions.

"To speak with a mind that 'compassionately cares for living beings as if they were our own babies' is Loving-Speech." We speak in a kindly voice to our children. But in an emergency a parent will shout a warning or a corrective. It often takes a raised voice to get someone's attention. This is also Loving-Speech.

Dogen writes, "We should study how Loving-Speech has power to transform the world." Our everyday language is debased. Advertisements bombard us with lies and false claims. Politicians and leaders carefully select compassionate-sounding words, but their first concerns are re-election, self-protection, and/or national chauvinism. When was the last time we heard a leader apologize for an injustice or violence imposed on their own citizens or another nation? But words can convey honesty, repentance, and generosity. Then they move the world towards peace. Narrowly crafted policy pronouncements are not Loving-Speech. Yet Loving-Speech is actually all around us. It is spoken by mothers and children, poets and writers. It actually goes beyond words to include music, dance, and silent prayer. Such speech is the source of our truest, most enduring power.

BENEFICIAL-ACTION

Beneficial-Action is the work of harmonizing self and the whole world. The Bodhisattva Avalokiteśvara has a thousand arms. Each hand wields a tool of liberation and each palm has its own discerning eye. Beneficial-Action means looking, listening, and helping without thinking about what we will get out of it. Dogen Zenji explains:

> Ignorant people may think that if we benefit
> others too much, our own benefit will be ex-
> cluded. This is not the case. Beneficial-Action
> is the whole of Dharma; it benefits both self
> and other widely.

Like Loving-Speech, Beneficial-Action is clearly an expression of Giving. It is not charity, though. In the West, charity is often motivated by two factors, the first a sense of moral or social obligation, *noblesse oblige*, and the second is the benefit, real or imagined, that accrues to oneself in return for an act of charity. Beneficial-Action is done simply for the sake of the action itself, without concern for any outcome or benefit.

In the Gospel of Matthew, Jesus tells his followers, "Love your enemies and pray for those who persecute you." Preaching on this verse, Martin Luther King Jr. said that in seeking to love one's enemy, one must...

> ...discover the element of good in one's enemy.
> And every time you begin to hate that person,
> realize that there is some good there and look
> at those good points which will over-balance
> the bad point...There is a recalcitrant South
> of our soul revolting against the North of our
> soul...

Dogen Zenji writes in the same spirit, but he extends Beneficial-Action to the whole earth and its elements.

> We should equally benefit friends and foes
> alike; we should benefit self and others alike...
> If we attain such a mind we can perform Ben-
> eficial-Action even for grass, trees, wind, and
> water.

Our meditation practice or *zazen* is the essence of Beneficial-Action. *Zazen* is selfless activity beyond the usual meaning of "good" and "bad." It is a rare kind of body-mind practice that transcends *karma*. As we harmonize our individual body and mind, *zazen* mysteriously harmonizes the whole world. Maybe there is no mystery. As each of us is at peace, those around us naturally resonate with the energy of peace. Peace ripples out in widening circles.

IDENTITY-ACTION

A great Bodhisattva lives in this suffering world with a vow to save all beings before saving herself. She or he may appear as a street person, as a soldier, as a bank teller, a mechanic, a prostitute, short-order cook, musician, preacher, mail carrier, or monk. The practice of Identity-Action entails the continuous reinvention of self. This is what Buddhists call "skillful means" or *upāya*, meeting each suffering being exactly as he or she needs to be met. Such a reinvention is neither pretense nor act. Using Identity-Action we reinvent ourselves according to our inborn Bodhisattva instinct.

This is the deepest of the Four Embracing Dharmas. While the Hebrew Scriptures teach Justice and the New Testament teaches Love, Buddhism teaches about Identity, the oneness of all being, and the difference of each interwoven existence. *Samanattata,* as it is used in the early Pali text quoted above, may be translated as cooperation, impartiality, or consistency. Dogen reaches further:

> Identity-Action means not to be different — neither different from self nor from others. For example, it is how, in the human world, the Tathāgata identifies himself with human beings. Because he identifies himself in the human world, we know that he must be the same in other worlds. When we realize Identity Action, self and others are one suchness.

Dogen's presentation on Identity-Action closes with a meditation on relations between a nation's people and their ruler.

> Because mountains do not refuse to be mountains, they can be mountains and reach great heights. Because wise rulers do not weary of their people they attract many people. "Many people" means a nation. "A wise ruler" may mean an emperor. Emperors do not weary of their people. This does not mean that they fail to offer rewards and punishments, but that they never tire of their people...Because wise rulers are clear, they do not weary of their people. Although people always desire to form a nation and to find a wise ruler, few of them fully understand the reason why a wise ruler is wise. Therefore, they are simply glad to be embraced by the wise ruler. They don't realize that they themselves are embracing a wise ruler. Thus the principle of Identity-Action exists both in the wise ruler and ignorant people.

Like much of Dogen's writing, this metaphor works on several levels at once. On one level, each of us, citizens in a national state, feels related to our president, prime minister, or king... whether we like it or not. On another level, our own body is kind of a nation. Mind is ruler, but for its own proper function it depends on the function of muscles, bones, and organs. When all elements are working together our body is healthy, even though we ourselves are never fully aware of how this functioning occurs. In this way, we ourselves are "the wise ruler and ignorant people."

Dogen's metaphor of governance is as much rooted in Confucian values as in buddhadharma. Yet it accords with his vision of Buddhism, offering both a critique and a directive about how to understand society. Identity-Action is simply an expression of what the ancestors called Dependent Origination. Because there is this, there is that. Because this arises, that arises. Together "this" arising and "that arising" make up an inseparable whole we conventionally call a nation. But each nation and each person is part of an endless tapestry of existence made of whole cloth. Katagiri Roshi said: "Differentiation must be formed not in differentiation, but in equality. Then, differentiation and equality are working in Identity-Action."

Like Confucius, Dogen was an idealist. But Dogen was unafraid to roll up the long sleeves of his robe. Confucius wrote, "When the perfect order prevails, the world is like a home shared by all." Soon after writing *Shishobo,* Dogen set out for the forests of Echizen province to build a great monastery, Eiheiji, his "Temple of Eternal Peace." Seven hundred years later, Eiheiji monks still blend with each other "like milk and water." The great trees and the long monastic halls embrace and dance together as Dogen would have wished. The Bodhisattvas rejoice.

4. "I KNOW JUST HOW YOU FEEL"

I came across a profound story in Taylor Branch's *Pillar of Fire*, the second book in his three-volume history of America in the age of Martin Luther King, Jr. Three civil rights workers — James Chaney, Andrew Goodman, and Mickey Schwerner — were murdered by the Ku Klux Klan in Neshoba County, Mississippi in June of 1964. Klan member Horace Burnette later gave a confession to the FBI. Burnette described the events of that terrible night. By the side of a country road Alton Wayne Roberts pulled Mickey Schwerner out of the rights workers' car. He put a gun to Schwerner's head, saying, "Are you that nigger lover?" Schwerner replied, "Sir, I know just how you feel." Schwerner and his co-workers were shot and buried beneath an earthen dam.

A Bodhisattva practices without regard for success or failure. Civil rights workers in Mississippi were thoroughly trained in the practice of nonviolence, which is in fact the Bodhisattva's Four Embracing Dharmas. Because he intuitively understood Identity-Action, Schwerner could say, "Sir, I know just how you feel." What did he mean? Did he understand Wayne Roberts' fear or his hatred? Were they, in fact Mickey Schwerner's own feelings? We will never know. Schwerner's compassionate response did not save his life, but the *karma* of his words is still unfolding. Because of his courage, a man confessed to these murders. We are still studying his words and actions, vowing to make them our own.

At the end of *Bodaisatta Shishobo,* Dogen writes, "Because each of these Four Embracing Dharmas includes all the Four Embracing Dharmas, there are Sixteen Embracing Dharmas." This is another way of expressing the interpenetrating nature of things. None of these practices exists apart from the others. Giving implies Loving-Speech, Beneficial-Action, and Identity-Action. Identity-Action is our true nature, bringing forth all the other Dharmas. And so on. Practicing one Dharma, we practice all four. Practicing all four Dharmas, we embrace all being, dancing with our head among the clouds of heaven and our feet stepping along the ocean's muddy bottom.

MINDFULNESS MUST BE ENGAGED

I had a broadside hanging over my desk at Buddhist Peace Fellowship in the early 1990s. It was a teaching by Thich Nhat Hanh titled "Mindfulness Must Be Engaged." Mindfulness is the key to our body, the key to our lives. But how is it engaged? Is this engagement part of our true understanding or is it something extra that is added on?

The Buddha's teachings on mindfulness invite us to be mindful of the body in the body, feelings in the feelings, breath in the breath. This means becoming aware of actions and things from within themselves. Aware that one is never truly apart from one's body, breath, feelings. In just this way we are engaged with the world, aware that we are never apart from it. There is no outside, or as an old Zen saying goes, "There is nowhere in the world to spit."

Explore this in meditation. Sit comfortably in an upright posture. Close your eyes and rest your hands lightly in your lap or on your knees. Take a deep breath in through your nose and mouth. Let the air fill your body, moving down from chest, expanding your lungs, until the breath reaches your *hara* or abdomen, a few inches below the navel. Now breathe out slowly and steadily through your mouth, following the contraction of your belly and the air as it moves through your mouth and back out into the wide world. Again, breathe in deeply through nose and mouth, then slowly breathe out. When you reach the end of this exhalation, push a little more air out of your lungs, then breathe in once more. Our usual breath leaves nearly a quarter of our lungs filled with stale air. This kind of breathing brings a refreshing change.

You can try this whenever you sit down to meditate, settling your mind and body into meditation from the start. Try it at work or before a meeting. It is a simple way to bring mind and body together, to ground our thoughts and feelings in breath. If you have some trouble on the out-breath, just begin again, without any judgment and soon you will be able to feel some control over your thoughts and over the muscles that control your breath.

Feel the air as it flows in and out of your body. Each breath brings life. When the motion of breath stops, life stops. And yet the air is everywhere, completely connected like a single seamless fabric spread across the world. The air you breathe this very moment is the same air that a woman sitting next to you is breathing. It is the same air breathed by a homeless man with a begging bowl on a downtown corner. It is the air that a mother and daughter are breathing as they sit in the hospital emergency room waiting to see a doctor.

Across the bay at San Quentin prison, four thousand men live a harsh life behind steel bars. The air they breathe smells of sea and fog, of sweat and closeness. I would be surprised if there is any among us whose life is not connected to someone behind bars — a friend, or relative, someone we write to or visit. Only circumstances and karma find some of us here in a park and others under lock and key. At root, our lives, our breath is the same.

The same air sustains Burmese refugees along the Thai border, people whose lives are just as precious to the world as our lives. People who have offered their dharma and teachers to us. I have seen these people, shared words and meals with them. Their children are as full of fun and promise as our children, but their futures are shadowed by war and disease.

Thousands of miles from here, the vast rain forests of Brazil are lungs for the planet, taking in carbon dioxide, exhaling the oxygen all beings need for life. Those Amazon Basin forests are disappearing at the rate of 20 square miles per day. Each year an area of forest the size of Massachusetts falls to fires and bulldozers. We are intimately dependent on the trees of Amazonia. Even now it is generating the air we need.

I have read that each breath we take contains atoms once breathed by Christ or Buddha, by Caesar or Hitler. Maybe this is apocryphal science. But the thought is compelling nonetheless. The energy we transmute through body into action is forever conserved. The physical molecules of breath and body are conserved. Form is endlessly changing. Buddhadharma teaches this, but we confirm it in our own experience. Nothing is lost. Mindfulness *must* be engaged because it *is* engaged. We can enjoy our breathing because countless beings are breathing and being with us. We suffer because countless beings suffer and we are not apart from them. Mindfulness is the complete awareness of interdependence. Awareness comes with responsibility — the ability to respond. No distinction of inside and outside. In this moment of silence just let us enjoy our breathing.

ACTIVE DHARMA: SOURCES OF SOCIALLY ENGAGED BUDDHISM

— **Donald Rothberg & Hozan Alan Senauke**

What is socially engaged Buddhism? It is dharma practice that flows from an understanding of the complete and endlessly complicated interdependence of all life. It is the practice of the bodhisattva vow to save all beings. It is to know that our liberation and the liberation of others are inseparable. It is to transform ourselves as we transform all our relationships and our larger society. It is working from the inside out and from the outside in, depending on needs and conditions. It is to see the world through the eye of Dharma and to respond empathically and actively.

Those of us on this path can draw on the past. While the history of Buddhism offers many exemplary movements and figures, here we briefly explore four key movements and leaders, identifying how each developed a core intention that deeply informs our engaged practice today.

We begin with the Indian movement of the Untouchables against systemic oppression based on caste, led in the first half of the 20th century by Dr. B.R. Ambedkar and continuing to this day. We then explore the Sarvodaya movement in Sri Lanka, founded by Dr. A. T. Ariyaratne, guided by a Gandhian vision of intertwining personal and community development based on shared work and practice. Thirdly, we focus on the Vietnamese Buddhist movement during the war and the work of Thich Nhat Hanh, Sister Chan Khong, and others to widen the scope of Buddhist practice, developing a deeply influential understanding of nondual social action and conflict transformation. Finally, we move to North America to examine the work of the Buddhist Peace Fellowship (BPF), growing from Robert Aitken Roshi's broad notion of decentralized and self-regulated Buddhist communities.

B.R. AMBEDKAR DIORAMA: AMBEDKAR
MUSEUM — NAGPUR, INDIA — 2010

RESPONDING TO INSTITUTIONALIZED OPPRESSION

Bhimrao R. Ambedkar was born in 1891 in central India, what is now Maharastra. Though his family came from the Hindu untouchable Mahar caste — subject to intense economic and social discrimination — Ambedkar's father, a noncommissioned officer in the Indian colonial army, found places for his children at the government school. But the terrible realities of discrimination meant that Mahar children were ignored by their teachers and literally compelled to sit outside the classroom. Ambedkar later reflected:

> My poor Untouchable brothers live in a condi-
> tion worse than the slaves. Slaves were at least
> touched by their lords. Our very touch has
> been deemed a sin. Not even a British govern-
> ment has been able to do anything for us.

Ambedkar was a brilliant student, and in 1907 he was among
the first untouchable youths to enter the University of Bombay, later receiving a fellowship to study political science at
Columbia University in New York. By the time he reestablished
himself in India, he held PhDs from Columbia and the London
School of Economics and had been admitted to the British Bar.
But Ambedkar was once again confronted with discrimination. Back in India upper-caste lawyers would not meet with
him. Clerks under his nominal direction would literally throw
files and papers on his desk. However, his reputation among
the untouchables, or Dalits (meaning "suppressed"), as they
were beginning to call themselves, was growing quickly.

Ambedkar's original public focus was on improving the
position of his people with regard to the British colonialism.
Over time, however, he came to see that the entrenched Hindu
caste system formed an almost insurmountable social and
economic obstacle for Dalits. Despite pious intentions and
legal reform, caste was not about to disappear from Hinduism.
So Ambedkar began a thorough study of world religions, seeking a spiritual path that would lead to social equality, while
also attempting to understand the religious roots of institutional oppression. At a 1935 Mahar rally he said, "I say to you,
abandon Hinduism and adopt any other religion which gives
you equality of status and treatment."

As India moved towards independence, Ambedkar was
often highly critical of Mahatma Gandhi's Congress Party.
Ambedkar's views were controversial, but he was an exemplary jurist and scholar. The Congress-led government invited
Ambedkar to serve as independent India's first law minister
and charged him with writing its new constitution.

By this time, Ambedkar had seriously turned his attention to Buddhism as an egalitarian faith native to India. He found the rigorous dialogue, process, and democratic basis of sangha life described in early Buddhism to be a solid grounding for India's new constitution. On presenting this constitution he wrote:

> Democracy's life is based on liberty, equality and fraternity; there is a total lack of equality in India. We have equality in politics, but inequality reigns in the sphere of society and economics. How can a people divided into thousands of castes and sub-castes be a nation? The way to grow strong and united is to remove all such barriers.

In 1956, Dr. Ambedkar converted to Buddhism, receiving the traditional Three Refuges and Five Precepts from a senior Buddhist monk in a public ceremony. Then Ambedkar turned around and offered the refuges and precepts to nearly 400,000 Dalits in attendance. However, six weeks following this historic mass conversion, he passed away, just three days after he had completed his abiding work, *The Buddha and His Dhamma.*

His untimely death left a void of leadership among the Dalits that took years to fill. Still, Ambedkar had reframed traditional Buddhism. By emphasizing its social teachings and clarifying karma as moral opportunity rather than fate, he offered a dharma that would clearly resonate with and uplift the oppressed and dispossessed.

His legacy can be seen in India among multitudes of ex-Untouchables and hundreds of communities and organizations, some highly political and some religious. An impressive nonsectarian network of Buddhist communities across India, called TBMSG (Trailokya Bauddha Mahasangha Sahayaka Gana), closely intertwines dharma and social service. TBMSG provides grassroots, indigenously led meditation retreats and Buddhist training for thousands of Dalits, many of whom live in urban slums. Meditation and practice inform TBMSG's social work, which includes childcare, schools, literacy projects, libraries, medical programs, and training for self-sufficiency and livelihood.

After nearly 30 years, a new generation of Dalit leaders is emerging in TBMSG, building new and confident dharma communities in India for the first time since Buddhism's decline there nearly a thousand years ago.

There have also been initial connections between Dalits and Buddhist people of color in the United States and an exchange of experiences and ways of practicing. Much like Martin Luther King Jr. and other civil rights leaders, Dr. Ambedkar saw the inseparability of spirituality and social liberation. His work is a powerful legacy for those of us now working to connect Buddhist practice and attention to various forms of oppression such as race, ethnicity, class, gender, and sexual orientation.

A.T. ARIYARATNE (SULAK SIVARAKSA IN THE
BACKGROUND): SRI LANKA — 1999

COMMUNITY DEVELOPMENT

If Ambedkar's vision was about linking spirituality to a movement for the rights of a downtrodden people, then Dr. A. T. Ariyaratne and the Sarvodaya movement point to the importance of what we might call community development.

Dr. Ariyaratne, or Ari, as he is familiarly known, was born in November 1931 in Galle, Sri Lanka. His middle-class family was devoted to education and Buddhism, and the young Ariyaratne advanced through school quickly. In 1956, he was hired as a science teacher at the prestigious Nalanda College.

In that first year, on his own, he surveyed the Rodiya communities of untouchables living in terrible poverty. The following year he visited rural Gandhian communities across India, meeting and traveling with Gandhi's famed disciple, Vinoba Bhave. Bhave had formed a nonviolent social movement based on giving, particularly giving land, for which he used the Gandhian term *sarvodaya*, meaning "the welfare of all." This combined social-spiritual vision deeply influenced Ariyaratne.

Returning to Sri Lanka, Ariyaratne reflected on how these principles might guide a form of communal action that he called *shramadana*, "a gift of labor." In December 1958, Ariyaratne, along with a group of Nalanda students and teachers, organized the first *shramadana* work camp in the Rodiya village of Kanatoluwa.

The volunteers worked with the villagers to survey the area, assess resources, discuss what needed to be done, and clarify the spiritual principles supporting the project. After the first work camp's success, requests for *shramadana* camps soon came from numerous impoverished villages. Each camp created new local infrastructures grounded in the empowerment of all involved. Ariyaratne was finding that his amalgam of Buddhist and Gandhian principles and practices was working very well, resulting in roads, clinics, and schools as well as empowerment and cooperation. The workers' motto was, "We build the road and the road builds us."

From these seeds, an organization — Sarvodaya — grew to become the largest grassroots development network in Sri Lanka. Today, this network comprises some 15,000 villages and 34 district offices.

Sarvodaya reframes the teaching of the Four Noble Truths, giving it a social interpretation designed to resolve community problems, asking, "What is the problem? What are the roots of the problem? What is the solution? How do we get there?"

The first truth, the truth of suffering and unsatisfactory conditions, translates as the fact of a village in trouble. Scholar George Bond writes, "This concrete form of suffering becomes the focus of mundane awakening. Villagers should recognize the problems in their environment such as poverty, disease, oppression, and disunity." Understanding the second truth, the origin of suffering, is to see the role of factors like greed, hatred, and selfishness.

The third truth is that the villagers' suffering can cease. The means to solve the problem lies in the fourth truth, the Eightfold Path. This truth encompasses all the shared abilities, wisdom, and efforts of the community, organized for its own liberation. Dr. Ariyaratne writes, "The struggle for external liberation is the struggle of internal liberation from greed, hatred, and ignorance, at the same time."

Sarvodaya has played a vital peacemaking role in the context of the violent civil war in Sri Lanka that erupted starting in 1983. It has carried out the difficult and dangerous work of creating connections across Buddhist Sinhalese and Hindu Tamil lines, creating a peace movement based on such connections, despite great risks.

At the first BPF Summer Institute in 1991, Ari told us how Sinhalese nationalists came into his home office one day with guns drawn, ready to kill him. His response was to say, "Well, you can do that if you wish to, but please explain to me how that is going to be a resolution to the suffering you've experienced." They left without harming him or anyone else.

Today more than 100,000 young people are involved in Shanti Sena, the nonviolent peace brigade responding to religious and communal strife. They have organized huge peace gatherings in the last 10 years; in 2002, some 650,000 people met and meditated together in support of the recently enacted peace accords and ceasefire.

Sarvodaya also played a huge and highly praised role in the wake of the December 2004 tsunami. Tens of thousands of volunteers brought material, psychological, and spiritual help to devastated villages, and are continuing to support their rebuilding.

The work of Dr. Ariyaratne and Sarvodaya has had a significant impact on many Western engaged Buddhists, in part through Ari's regular visits to BPF and other sanghas in North America. Dharma teacher Joanna Macy, for example, spent a year with Sarvodaya in 1979–80, which deeply impacted her own highly influential work in developing groups, organizations, and communities able to transform the pain of the world, as well as in articulating social interpretations of many core Buddhist teachings.

NONDUAL ACTION IN THE MIDST OF WAR

An "engaged" approach to Buddhism in Vietnam goes back more than 1,000 years. This history is often connected with the defense of the country and the people, and offers many examples of engagement as a place of practice, liberation, and social change. Hence, when a new wave of engaged Buddhism emerged in the 1930s, in large part aiming to end French colonialism (France had invaded Vietnam in 1858), there was considerable historical resonance.

According to Thich Minh Duc, a senior monk now settled in California, the engaged movement in Vietnam had three broad phases. The first, starting in the 1930s, was called "Buddhism for Everybody." The intention was to bring Buddhist teachings and practices out of the monasteries, to help guide daily life.

The second, starting in the 1950s in the midst of war, was called "Buddhism Goes into the World." This was expressed especially through service — to meet the basic needs of the people, particularly refugees, for shelter, food, education, and medical care.

The third phase, "Getting Involved," started after the government crackdown on Buddhism in 1963 and involved explicit activism, intended especially to stop the war and the persecution of Buddhists.

Thich Nhat Hanh, born in 1926, participated in all three phases. After entering the Tu Hieu monastery in Hue at 17, he soon rebelled against the limited monastic curriculum and moved to Saigon, where he could connect traditional Buddhism with the exploration of contemporary literature and philosophy.

In the 1950s and early 1960s, he founded or co-founded a number of organizations, including several centers of Buddhist studies and activism, the School of Youth for Social Service, and the Tiep Hien Order, for practitioners of engaged Buddhism. He also was very involved in speaking and acting against the war.

After his 1966 Western speaking tour — during which he met Thomas Merton and Martin Luther King Jr., influencing significantly King's decision to speak out against the war in 1967 — Thich Nhat Hanh was advised by Buddhist leaders in Vietnam not to return, for fear of assassination or imprisonment. He was forced to begin life in exile.

In the years since then, he and a number of collaborators, particularly his disciple Sister Chan Khong, have articulated a highly influential interpretation of engaged Buddhism centered on a nondual approach to transforming conflicts. This approach, on our interpretation, has six basic elements:

Identifying the dualistic system of conflict: These Buddhist leaders pointed to the roots of the war as the struggle between apparent polar opposites, communists versus capitalists, a struggle that reflected the projections of the superpowers onto Vietnam. Their intention was to transform this oppressive system of conflict, which they saw as the source of immense suffering.

Not taking sides: Their strategy was to avoid both extremes, pointing beyond the dualistic conflict. They did not posit either side as "enemy" or "oppressor." According to Thich Nhat Hanh:

> The Vietnam War was, first and foremost, an ideological struggle. To ensure our people's survival, we had to overcome both communist and anticommunist fanaticism and maintain the strictest neutrality. Buddhists tried their best to speak for all the people and not take sides, but we were condemned as "pro-communist neutralists."

Grounding in the ethics of nonharming: Their commitment to nonviolence expressed the basic Buddhist ethical precepts and led to a strategy for peacemaking through ending the cycles of violence.

Responding to suffering: Their focus was in large part to respond to suffering — of the people, of the war, and of the two sides. Thich Nhat Hanh comments: "We were able to understand the suffering of both sides, the Communists and the anti-Communists. We tried to be open to both...to be one with them."

Not taking sides does not mean not responding: Through their actions, they showed that nondualism does not mean standing aside. They rebuilt homes and schools, dispensed medical care, set up clinics, helped refugees, and demonstrated to end the conflict.

The aim is reconciliation, not victory: Their long-term intention was not defeat of the "enemy" but rather, reconciliation. These efforts required considerable patience. Thich Minh Duc comments:

We did not think that by demonstrating we'd turn things around immediately. Rather, we had to look to the long-term process of practice (*tu*). *Tu* means to transform bad to good — today one inch, tomorrow another inch... For 100 years, we were controlled by the French. We knew that it would take years to untie the knot.

ROBERT AITKEN: HAWAII — 2001

A Network of Communities

BPF was born in 1978 on the back porch of Robert Aitken Roshi's Maui Zendo. It was a gathering of practitioners who were appalled by American proxy wars in Central America and by the flourishing Cold War arms race. Originally, their idea was to organize a chapter of the nonviolent Fellowship of Reconciliation (FOR). But FOR, which has separate fellowships for different faiths, suggested that they start a "Buddhist Peace Fellowship." Cofounders Nelson Foster, Robert and Anne Aitken, and other local Zen friends were soon joined by many Western Buddhists drawn to social engagement, including Gary Snyder, Joanna Macy, Jack Kornfield, Tai Unno, Al Bloom, Ryo Imamura, and others.

By the time BPF began, Aitken had been an activist for decades, speaking out on labor issues, nuclear disarmament, and opposition to war. For some years he was a tax resister. His Buddhist practice originated during three years in an internment camp in Japan during World War II. By chance, the well-known teacher and translator R. H. Blyth was interned in the same camp, and in the course of their captivity, Aitken received a vivid introduction to Zen, haiku, and literature in general.

After the war, Aitken took up Zen practice with Nyogen Senzaki in Los Angeles, and he went to Japan to study Zen in the early 1950s. In 1959 Robert and Anne Aitken founded what was to become the Diamond Sangha in their home in Honolulu, which continues to be Koko-An Zendo.

Aitken's study of anarchist writing — Proudhon, Kropotkin, Landauer, Emma Goldman, and many others — reinforced his belief in personal autonomy, decentralization, and spiritual community. These are principles that are also the essence of Buddhist sangha, as he has written:

> The traditional Sangha serves as a model for
> enterprise in this vision. A like-minded group
> of five can be a Sangha. It can grow to a modest

size, split into autonomous groups and then network. As autonomous lay Buddhist associations, these little communities will not be Sanghas in the classical sense, but will be inheritors of the name and of many of the original intentions. They will also be inheritors of the Base Community movements in Latin America and the Philippines — Catholic networks that are inspired by traditional religion and also by 19th-century anarchism.

Aitken's intention for BPF was not the creation of a new mass organization or religious order but a web of like-minded Buddhist activists. In its early years BPF was a loose ecumenical network linked by friendship and common purpose, with members clustered especially in Hawaii and the San Francisco Bay Area. Within three years the network had grown to several hundred members, moved its office to Berkeley, hired a part-time coordinator, formed the first chapters, organized several conferences and meetings, and begun publishing a newsletter that later became *Turning Wheel.* Local BPF chapters still function with great autonomy, bound by their mutual practice.

This web of sanghas is a small step in the direction of what Aitken Roshi calls Buddhist Anarchism, which itself is a small step towards the healthy remaking of society. Aitken frequently cites the old Wobbly [Industrial Workers of the World] motto: "Build the new within the shell of the old."

Aside from addressing the pressing realities of U.S. militarism and the encroachment of an all-devouring corporate capitalism, BPF early on was drawn to matters of religious freedom and human rights in Asia. In the first BPF newsletters, one reads about the plight of Buddhists in Tibet, Vietnam, and Bangladesh. And just as we are still wrestling with the depredations of militarism and global capitalism, it is interesting to see we have many of the same international concerns today as 30 years ago.

BPF has grown from that initial vision as straight and true as we could manage. The network of decentralized communities remains, and BPF's Buddhist Alliance for Social Engagement (BASE) program, founded by Diana Winston and named to reflect affinity with the Catholic Base Community movement, has organized or facilitated more than 30 six-month trainings for small autonomous groups of practitioners. BPF's many other projects have included working in prisons, organizing youth, investigating race and diversity, and seeding social activism in countless Buddhist centers and sanghas in America.

* * *

BPF and all of us on the line of change draw strength from the history of modern engaged Buddhist communities including those led by Dr. Ambedkar, Dr. Ariyaratne, and Thich Nhat Hanh. Its mission is limitless, like the bodhisattva vows themselves.

POSTSCRIPT

Robert Baker Aitken — Dairyu Chotan/Great Dragon (of the) Clear Pool — died on August 5, 2010, in Honolulu at the age of 93. Aitken Roshi was a prophetic and inconvenient voice right to the end. I have a picture of him from a year or two back, smiling impishly, holding up hand-lettered sign reading: The System Stinks. Aitken Roshi never saw an inch of separation between his vision of justice and the reality of complete interdependence. The vast universe, with all its joys and sorrows was his true dwelling place. It still is. Aitken Roshi, *presente*!

WHAT IS TO BE DONE?

What is to be done? These words, translated from Russian, are the title of Lenin's famous 1902 polemic on the development of a revolutionary movement, something I studied long ago. Similar words are frequently spoken in the Pali suttas when the Buddha helps a disciple to the revolutionary ground of enlightenment. "What must be done has been done!" And today, now months after September 11, anthrax scares, bombing in Afghanistan, the Taliban's fall, and open-ended hostilities, many of us are still asking, "What is to be done?"

Seeds planted earlier in life germinate when proper conditions arise. This is a fact beyond good or bad, right or wrong. We live in the conditional world of *samsara.* In Zen practice we try to remember what is originally known — that *samsara* and *nirvana* are not separate. Remembering, realizing this is the hard work of Zen. So here I hesitantly offer these conditional and still-forming views. Shakyamuni Buddha teaches us that "right view" or *samma-ditthi* is the ending of attachment to views. This is both path and goal. In either case, I am still on that long road.

The unfolding events of these last months haunt my dreams. Images of the World Trade Center and the Pentagon are etched in my mind. A jet passing overhead calls it all up again. The Taliban has supposedly been defeated, but the bombing of Afghanistan has created more refugees and victims from among the world's poorest people, people who themselves were the Taliban's victims. The destabilization of Afghanistan and neighboring countries affected by U.S.-led military strife carries unthinkable but real risks of nuclear weapons. There are times when the sorrow of it all nails me to the spot. And yet we have to keep moving forward on the path. How shall we do that?

There are some principles or practices that I find very useful, borrowed from the Bernie Glassman's Zen Peacemaker Order and the Peacemaker Community. Their three tenets are:

Not-knowing, giving up fixed ideas about ourselves and the universe;
Bearing witness to the joy and suffering of the world;
Loving actions towards ourselves and others.

"Not-knowing" is deeply challenging for us. It means letting go of one's own sense of righteousness and fear, and being willing not to have the answers. It calls for patient endurance. At the same time not-knowing calls us to recognize all points of view: the views of George Bush, Osama Bin Laden, His Holiness the Dalai Lama, Jerry Falwell, our neighbor, the person sitting next to us on the bus. Each person's view, however we might recoil from it, fully expresses life in this world of causes and conditions. And within ourselves is the human potential to embody each view.

"Bearing witness" is about seeing oneself in intimate relationship with beings. This relationship is so awesome that the proper response is to sit down and become fully receptive. To sit quietly and pay attention. Zazen. One meaning of bearing witness is that we must bear or endure what we see and hear. Avalokitesvara Bodhisattva is the hearer of the cries of the world. We try to be like her. So we go to the places in the world and in our body-mind where suffering and joy manifest, to see and learn as much as we can about causes and conditions. To touch the common identity we all share.

Bearing witness also means to study the suffering of all beings and to find where that suffering lives right in my own body and mind. This goes hand in hand with not knowing. We bear witness to the falling WTC towers, and the thousands of people who died there. We bear witness to Afghan women suffering under Taliban oppression, and to the suffering of the Taliban themselves. We bear witness to the simple joys that persist in our lives, like grass pushing up through cracks in the sidewalk.

A further meaning of bearing witness is to carry our witness to others, to help people see life as we see it. And to see things as they see them. We have an opportunity to forge links with people from other faiths. To visit neighborhood mosques and temples, to open our eyes to life in countries where people don't have the wealth and hi-tech machines many of us share. The responsibility of bearing witness flows from seeing reality as it is.

"Healing ourselves and others" is the third tenet. These tenets and practices never move in a linear fashion. Each one is constantly informing the others. Healing proceeds from inside to outside, then back again. Healing is what happens as one sits in the meditation hall watching the tide of feelings and thought. It is creating circles where our friends and community speak about what we are experiencing. It is writing to our leaders, organizing or participating in silent vigils and demonstrations. The Quakers call this "speaking truth to power."

We are trying to bring forth the Buddha's teaching of peace. In the *Dhammapada*, Verse 5 the Buddha said, "Hatred (or hostility) is never appeased by hatred in this world; by non-hatred alone is hatred appeased. This is an Eternal Law." Terrorism, the violence of bombs, the structural violence of starvation will bear fruit in more violence. Ending our own violence and violence in society is the path to healing. Can we take a stand that is _both_ strong and kind? Can our vision and language include all suffering people, including ourselves, without falling into a warm and fuzzy all-sidedness?

Thich Nhat Hanh writes, "You have to work for the survival of the other side if you want to survive yourself. It is really very simple. Survival means survival of humankind as a whole, not just part of it." When we engage honestly, fearlessly with friends, foes, and ourselves, we are risking peace. Then we know we are completely alive.

Dogen's "Genjo Koan" ends with the following story.

Zen master Boache of Mt. Mayu was fanning himself. A monk approached and said, "Master, the nature of wind is permanent and there is no place it does not reach. Why, then, do you fan yourself?"

"Although you understand that the nature of the wind is permanent," Baoche replied, "you do not understand the meaning of its reaching everywhere."

"What is the meaning of it reaching everywhere?" asked the monk again. The master just kept fanning himself. The monk bowed deeply.

What is to be done? Even though all beings without exception are Buddha, we *still* must realize it. Fanning is necessary practice, our work of realization. And fanning keeps the wind of Buddha nature in constant circulation, so inherent realization may manifest for all — Americans, Afghans, Israelis, Palestinians, Indians, Pakistanis, and so on — irrespective of faith, culture, race, class, gender. Our work is to keep fanning. By our efforts, by our practice, winds of change rise in the wilderness of our suffering, and reach everywhere.

— 3.1.02

NOTES TOWARD A PRACTICAL ZEN PSYCHOLOGY

Do I contradict myself?
Very well then I contradict myself,
(I am large, I contain multitudes.)
I concentrate toward them that are nigh, I wait on the door-slab.

— Walt Whitman, from "Song of Myself"

Thirteen hundred years ago at Nan Hua Temple in China, when Master Huineng, the Sixth Zen Ancestor, taught his verses of "Formless Repentance" he offered an unusual version of the Bodhisattva's Four Vows.

> The sentient beings of our own minds are numberless, and we vow to save them all. The afflictions of our own minds are limitless, and we vow to eradicate them all. The teachings of our own minds are inexhaustible, and we vow to learn them all. The enlightenment of buddhahood of our own minds is unsurpassable, and we vow to achieve it.

Huineng's first vow goes to the root of practice. "The sentient beings of our own minds are limitless, and we vow to save them all." This is my personal work, each person's work. Like

Whitman, "I am large, I contain multitudes." The Theravadan scholar Nyanaponika Thera writes:

> There are within us countless seeds for new lives, for innumerable potential "beings," all of whom we should vow to liberate from the wheel of *samsara*, as the Sixth Zen Patriarch expressed it.
>
> — *The Vision of Dhamma*

Then, in a footnote he speculates:

> This may be a somewhat ironical reference by that great sage to the fact that the well-known Mahayanic Bodhisattva vow of liberating all beings of the universe is often taken much too light-heartedly by many of his fellow Mahayanists.

Maybe so, but at our temple, the Bodhisattva Vows are chanted again and again in our monthly precept recitation, after every dharma talk, as an element of many ceremonies. We use a more common formulation: "Sentient beings are numberless; I vow to save them." I don't think these vows are taken lightly.

I am not a psychologist; I don't even play one on television. But as a 21st Century Zen person I have to translate the teachings of ancient buddhas and ancestors to stay on the path day by day. Eight hundred years ago, Japanese Zen master Dogen wrote:

> To study the Buddha Way is to study the self. To study the self is to forget the self. To forget the self is to be enlightened by all things.
>
> — *Genjokoan*

Psychology is literally the study of self, of spirit. The last hundred years — since Freud and many creative souls after him threw the light of awareness into the hidden corners of consciousness — could be called the Age of Psychology. Though Freud might be spinning in his grave, psychology has become the pillar of most religion in the West. Western Buddhism has been so impacted by psychology that it is not always easy to see where religious praxis ends and therapy begins. As a Zen teacher I listen to students' suffering. Much of that suffering is rooted in old wounds, habits, and patterns. One could call that karma or neurosis. It depends on what lens one looks through.

Buddhism itself is a collection of psychological systems, its wisdom and practices evolving variously across ages, nations, and cultures. The Buddha's discovery of Dependent Origination, *paticasamupadda*, is about the system and workings of mind. Buddhadasa Bhikkhu, the late Thai teacher, describes Dependent Origination and rebirth, unfolding moment by moment. "Grasping and attachment will give rise to becoming and birth." In that moment of becoming and birth, which takes place in my mind, a "sentient being of my mind" is born, someone very close whom I must take care of.

Several hundred years later, the Yogācāra or Vijnanavada School arose as a vital expression of Mahayana Buddhism. This school located truth in mind or consciousness (*vijñāna*), rather than in things of the phenomenal world. Yogacara philosophers posited an enduring transpersonal consciousness called *ālaya vijñāna* (or Store-House Consciousness), where the karmic seeds of all our past action reside, ready to bloom in the present and future. This school greatly influenced Buddhist traditions of Northern and Eastern Asia, particularly the Zen schools. It also became a matter of debate and a touchstone for other doctrinal developments.

These approaches, along with that of other Buddhist and Taoist schools, are clear in the teachings of Huineng, Dogen, and all the great figures of Zen from China to Japan to America. But a painted rice cake doesn't fill my belly. Such theories and systems themselves don't dispel suffering. How can we save the suffering beings of our minds? How can I be of use to myself? Further, how do I study myself so that when I meet others — and when I meet myself — my own traumas and self do not block the path of liberation? The opportunities are numberless. For example:

• Waiting for a doctor's bad news; living with a serious chronic illness;
• Feeling helpless with a self-destructive friend or family member, or being a citizen of a self- and other-destructive nation.
• Enduring unjust accusations, or (maybe worse) *just* accusations;
• Losing my temper with a suffering but exasperating student, even when I have every intention to stay cool;
• Disagreeing with my teacher, or finding that my teacher disagrees with me;
• Wondering if I have the capacity bear the extent of another's suffering — am I willing to take it in?

A man of about fifty who practices regularly in our sangha sits down across from me. We sit upright, almost knee-to-knee. After numerous attempts at reconciliation and accommodation, he has left his marriage and the home he and his wife have shared for twenty years. As we talk, he weeps. There are two young children in the picture, and for the last several weeks, his wife has not allowed him to see them. They are in conflict about money, child visitation, ownership of their house, and about how to proceed towards divorce. "I didn't think it could ever come to this," he says. "I'm angry all the time. How can she keep me from seeing my own kids? And what is she telling them about me?" Tears are streaming down his face, falling freely on the black cushion he sits on. "Every conversation or note leaves me furious. I never knew I had such anger in me."

Lets step back and consider a way to understand this story. According to traditional Buddhist "cosmology" beings are born and live in six realms. Three lower realms are inhabited by:

1. Hungry ghosts or *pretas* — Their existence is marked by insatiable hunger and greed. Often they are depicted with swollen bellies and impossibly long, narrow necks.
2. Animals — Their characteristic is stupidity and prejudice. (Apologies to animal lovers who know better!)
3. The Hell realm, *naraka,* is marked by hatred and aggression. It is a place of ceaseless conflict. Beings live there until their past negative karma is used up.

There are three higher realms.

4. Demigods or *asuras* are sometimes known as fighting demons — envious, fiercely competitive, delighting in war and chaos. In past lives as humans they might have held good intentions, but nonetheless harmed others.
5. The *Deva* realm is a heavenly place, home to powerful beings who enjoy great but transient pleasures. Inhabitants are complacent, self-centered, and addicted to their pleasures.
6. The human realm (in which you are reading this right now) is our temporary home. Although it is marked by desire, passions, and doubt, it is also the realm within which one can fully awaken to the Buddha's wisdom. This is our great opportunity for freedom.

There are actually countless realms within this *saha* world of ours — *saha* translates as "the world to be endured" — and within the limitless world of our own mind. These six provide a useful but general template. One can consider these numberless realms as states of mind...pun intended. They have territoriality, a certain lifespan, and a wide influence on other states of mind, which are ceaselessly arising. The sentient beings of my mind necessarily affect the sentient beings of another's mind. The ripples of thoughts and feelings extend, reinforcing and conflicting among us as widening circles that create family, community, society, even heavens and hells.

When certain emotions come up — say the anger and resentment that man feels as he faces a crumbling marriage — in that very moment a sentient being of one's mind is reborn in a realm of suffering. In the anger he feels about a crumbling marriage and separation from his children, he might be reborn in a hell realm — the common hell realm of divorce, where one writhes around and sees no daylight of peace and harmony between partners who once loved each other. If he gives free rein to this being, it will make a mess. There is a powerful habitual tendency to project one's suffering outward and blame others for what one is feeling. Each sentient being embodies potentialities for complete enlightenment and terrible depravity. This simply seems to come with having a body. In an early sermon, Martin Luther King Jr. wrote:

> There is something within each of us that causes us to cry out with Goethe, "There is enough stuff in me to make both a gentleman and a rogue."

Between teacher and student, between self and self one must learn the most basic way to help. I heard my Zen teacher friend Darlene Cohen say, "Sometimes all you can do is hold hands with each other while you both go to hell."

If my training is sufficient and if I am quick enough, there is a space for practice that precedes the birth of a sentient being of my mind. The Buddhist teacher Ken McLeod describes the cause of suffering, the second of Shakyamuni's Four Noble Truths, as "emotional reactivity." Note: this is not emotion itself. So long as human beings have bodies and minds, emotions will always arise. Suppression leads to what Freud called "the return of the repressed," an almost inevitable and unpredictable experience of suffering in a future time and place. Repression itself is a kind of emotional reactivity. "Reactivity" is what happens after an emotion arises. We reject it, push it away violently. We blame others for causing what we feel. Or we cling to a feeling, believe it is real, desperately holding on for dear life. In the thrall of emotional reactivity, we are apt to assert — silently or out loud — "This is my truth," as if it were the rock upon which Moses stood, rather than a flimsy raft on a stormy sea. If one can simply accept emotion as it comes up, shining a light of awareness on it, then emotions, thoughts, sensations, etc. are free to fall way as easily as they arose. If not, if we see reaction as a hardened truth, then a sentient being is born in one's mind. Seen through the lens of the Buddha's law of Dependent Origination, this is just one turning of the wheel of birth and death. Ajahn Buddhadasa writes that Dependent Origination (or *paticcasamuppada*) is:

> ...a momentary and sudden matter, not an eternal matter. Therefore, the word *jati*, to be born must refer to birth in the moment of one revolution of Dependent Origination in the daily life of ordinary people, which is to say when mindfulness is absent...It's easy to know: when greed, anger, or delusion arise, then the self is born in one "life" already.

Meanwhile, it may seem I am treading close to Buddhist heresy, raising the banner of self, when the understanding and work of Zen, and all of the Buddha's teaching, points to its unreality. Self has a compounded nature. Past and present circumstances of mind and physical reality create an impermanent "thing" that I provisionally call the self. Yes, it is empty of "own being" or essence I can point to, but that is not to say that self is nonexistent. The challenge of dharma practice is to manifest True Self or Big Mind, taking responsibility for self, and for all the momentary selves that come and go on the ever-whirling wheel of birth and death. Another way to say this is that I take my words and actions seriously, but I try not to take myself too seriously. There is always room for a joke, or a wry, quizzical look at things. If a bumper sticker can be a field of spiritual truth, there is one on my Toyota van that says, "Don't believe everything you think."

So, back to the matter at hand. Sentient beings of my own mind are limitless: I vow to save them all. Once a being is born in my mind, then what? If it has come to this point, then saving this being, like any other suffering being walking to and fro in this world or in my mind, means turning towards it with what Dogen Zenji called "parental mind" or *roshin*.

> *Roshin* is the mind or attitude of a parent...A parent, irrespective of poverty or difficult circumstances, loves and raises a child with care. How deep is love like this? Only a parent can understand it. A parent protects the children from the cold and shades them from the hot sun with no concern for his or her own personal welfare. Only a person in whom this mind has arisen can understand it, and any one in whom this attitude has become second nature can fully realize it. — Dogen, *Tenzo Kyokun*

This explains how we take can care of our suffering selves. It is a way of re-parenting ourselves. When a sentient being arises in my mind, I have to take care of it for its whole life. Sometimes that life may be just a few minutes. Sometimes it is a span of hours or days. If the wound is deep, a traumatized being may stay around for years, lurking in the corners of one's mind, leaping painfully to life when conditions are in place. But however long a sentient being dwells in my mind, I vow not to abandon it.

Parents don't abandon children. Neither does a mother or father allow a child to do whatever it wants. For the sake of safety, limits and boundaries are set. But, the underlying principle of these boundaries is unconditional love, not domination. In dharma terms this means seeing each being as Buddha. Of course, this is often easier said than done.

Yesterday I had a series of frustrating and unpleasant telephone conversations, trying to deal with a glitch in my health insurance coverage. Each conversation entailed transfer to another faceless person, with long intervals of insipid music between bureaucrats. The music, intended to soothe, had the opposite effect. I got more and more angry, noting the impulse to globalize my sense of personal injustice, as in the old IWW motto, "An injury to one is an injury to all!" So as I waited and talked and waited and argued, a sentient being was birthed in my mind. In this case, it was an *asura*, or fighting demon, a being with good intentions, caught by aggression and anger. When I came to the unsatisfactory end of the line — at least for the day — I wanted to slam the phone into its cradle. I stopped to breathe and notice what was going on in my body. My chest was tight, my hands were shaking slightly, and there was an unsettled, slightly nauseated feeling in my stomach. A newborn demon was struggling for control.

At that moment, fighting back was fruitless. Yelling at insurance company employees — much as I wanted to — was going to be unproductive. I have learned that the hard way. Pretending there was no fighting demon in my own head was impossible, because it is not just mind over matter. When a being is born — out of stress, emotion, sickness, psychological or physiological imbalance — our nervous system reacts (another aspect of emotional reactivity), generating powerful neurotransmitters and hormones, that flow freely throughout the body. Asserting the obvious, because mind and body are inseparable, bodily activities (including zazen) affect mind, and mental activities strongly influence the body. The lifespan of a sentient being of my mind is directly linked to the presence of these neurochemicals in my body. Psychologist Paul Ekman calls what I am describing a "refractory" state.

For a while we are in a refractory state, during which time our thinking cannot incorporate information that does not fit, maintain, or justify the emotion we are feeling. This refractory state may be of more benefit than harm if it is brief, lasting for only a second or two...Difficulties can arise or inappropriate emotional behavior may occur when the refractory period lasts much longer, for minutes or perhaps even hours. A too-long refractory period biases the way we see the world and ourselves.

Whether I see this phenomenon in Buddhist or in modern psychological terms, after getting off the phone shaking and angry, I simply had to take care of myself, using tools of mindfulness, compassion, and patience. Sitting quietly I could feel the fear and grief underneath my initial reaction. What if I lose my insurance and can't afford medical care? What if my chronic health problems flare up now, and my life is threatened? Alarming fantasies come very quickly. If I acknowledge them, I can experience a slight softening. But a child's insistent clinging returned. This was not going to be so simple. It was necessary to meet this new being on a physical level. So I took a hot shower and sat zazen for a short period. The fighting demon slipped away, having had a blessedly short life. I felt a great relief. At the same time I knew that a "seed" of this demon-being lay planted in the rich soil of my Store-House Consciousness, requiring only the proper stimulus and nutriments to come back to life.

* * *

Dogen Zenji often returned to a verse from the *Lotus Sutra*: "Only a buddha together with a buddha can fathom the reality of all existence." We have a choice. We can allow these beings to torment us, seeing them as somehow outside of our self. Or we can see them as suffering bodhisattvas, who can teach us important lessons.

There are countless ways to save suffering beings wherever they make their home. Zazen itself includes the full experience of body and mind. Zazen is as indefinable as love or friendship. No matter how I may try to analyze it, or break it down into elements and particular practices, I can't get my mind around zazen. It includes all dharma systems — the perfections, the factors of enlightenment, the foundations of mindfulness, and so on — but is not limited by them. And it includes all sentient beings, who may arise momentarily and fade with the next breath. Zazen itself cultivates our capacity to see all beings — seemingly inside or outside — as Buddha.

Encountering suffering, zazen has an alchemical quality. Alchemy, the mystical study of transformation, appeared in cultures across the world from earliest times. Among its goals were universal life free from all illness, and the search for an *alkahest*, or universal solvent, which would dissolve all compounded things, freeing up the energy of transformation. In the vast circle of zazen one meets each being just as it is, accepts it, and lets it go freely on its way. Sometimes zazen rests on the breath — breathing in, meeting and accepting; breathing out, setting free. This is how one practices at the bedside of a friend who is sick or dying, holding her hand, breathing in alignment with her. If that kind of attention is enough and the moment of suffering passes, so be it. If a suffering being is more persistent, my effort will, of course, be more focused. That suffering being of my mind will become the object of my attention. What does this suffering look like, where does it live in my body, what is the specific quality of pain it brings? What does this being need? Not what does it *say* it needs, or what it cries out for or against, but what does it truly need in order to be free? Often this is not immediately obvious. But if I keep turning towards rather than away, the alchemical power of zazen, the pure spirit of inquiry, of asking how, will sooner or later dissolve suffering, allowing the mystery of change to take place.

In the diverse religions of ancients, mystery and miracle are one and the same. There is transformation. Demons become protectors, hungry ghosts feed the hungry, gods come down to earth and bring us peace. *"Do I contradict myself? Very well then I contradict myself."* And human beings wake up right in the middle of the whole catastrophe (a word whose Greek root implies "turning over"). In this *saha* world everything is turning, everything is burning. But if we can breathe freely and heal the numberless sentient beings of our own mind — never abandoning them, never turning away — then we will simply be awake. If, as Whitman writes, "I concentrate toward them that are nigh, I wait on the door-slab," I may intuitively see just how to help people meet their own suffering. Liberation will ripple across the universe.

NOVICE MONK: SHWEDAGON PAGODA —
RANGOON, BURMA — DECEMBER 2007

GRACE UNDER PRESSURE — BURMA'S SANGHA AFTER THE CRACKDOWN

Fearlessness may be a gift but perhaps more precious is the courage acquired through endeavor, courage that comes from cultivating the habit of refusing to let fear dictate one's actions, courage that could be described as "grace under pressure" — grace which is renewed repeatedly in the face of harsh, unremitting pressure.
— Aung San Suu Kyi, from *Freedom From Fear*

The rains of late September fell on the flash and flare of a hundred thousand saffron robes in the streets of Burma. The world's eye turned toward Burma, and toward monks chanting the *Sutra of Lovingkindness* as they marched down rainswept streets, turning their minds and prayers toward democracy and the nonviolent transformation of the military regime that has ruled Burma for forty-five years. Once again Burmese monks had taken up the practice of *patam nikkujjana kamma*, turning over their alms bowls, refusing alms from the military junta and their families, ritually denying the junta leaders refuge from the destructive karma of their own greed and brutality. In Burma, where monks and nuns are deeply trained in meditation, scholarship, and in peaceful acceptance of life's sufferings, this is an extraordinary act. As the novelist Ernest Hemingway defined courage, this is "grace under pressure."

On September 22nd monks surged through barriers blocking off opposition NLD leader Aung San Suu Kyi's home in Rangoon. Still under house arrest, Suu came outside to receive their blessings. They turned toward her and chanted:

> May we be completely free from all danger.
> May we be completely free from all grief.
> May we be completely free from poverty.
> May we have peace in heart and mind.

As monks took to the streets in greater numbers, they were flanked by thousands of ordinary Burmese. This was more than the junta could stand. On September 26th protest leaders — ordained and lay — were arrested. Burmese troops and the paramilitary Union Solidarity and Development Association blockaded the Shwedagon Pagoda and began to beat hundreds of people trapped on the temple grounds. Meanwhile monks and nuns continued to march through Rangoon's downtown, where they were attacked with bamboo canes. The following day troops fired on nearly fifty thousands people protesting in

Rangoon. How many were killed in this crackdown? We will never know. The beaten body of a monk was found floating in the Rangoon River, and this image was telegraphed around the world. The U.N.'s Special Rapporteur Paulo Sérgio Pinheiro reported that during the crackdown, a government-controlled crematorium had been running late in the night. He wrote:

> ...the Ye Way crematorium under the control of the Police Controller and Central Department, where credible sources report a large number of bodies (wrapped in plastic and rice bags) were burned during the night, between 4 a.m. and 8 a.m., on 27-30 September. Sources indicate that it was not usual practice for the crematorium to operate during the hours in question, that normal employees were instructed to keep away, and that the facility was operated on those nights by State security personnel or State-supported groups. At least one report indicates that some of the deceased being cremated had shaved heads and some had signs of serious injuries.

In the next days, in the wake of murder, beatings, and confusion, monasteries were emptied, locked and barricaded. Some monks were arrested, some forcibly disrobed, some dismissed to their home villages, and some fled. This was not the first time in Burma's history that monks have led protests, nor the first time they were attacked by the junta. But the junta's systematic violence against the Burmese *sangha* — revered as sons of Buddha — was unprecedented. The whole world could see it at last.

* * *

THE ROOTS OF THE SAFFRON REVOLUTION

Burma's population is 90% Theravada Buddhist, so the more than 400,000 monks and 75,000 nuns represent the most stable, ongoing institution of national life. Historically they have always played a role in society. Monks led the first anti-colonial activities in Burma when British officers entered temples with their shoes on. In the 1920s and 30s, as the anti-colonial movements grew, articulate monks like U Ottama and U Wissara spent long years in British prisons for their nationalist stance. U Wissara died in prison on the 167th day of a hunger strike. In 1988 and again in 1990, monks helped lead the democracy movement. Many were shot, many more imprisoned, with more than ninety still in custody when the recent protests began.

Theravada monastics live in close relationship to the wider community. Their response to Burma's extreme economic hardship is, in a sense, logical. If the people cannot eat, monks and nuns cannot eat.

The Orwellian military regime, established in 1962 by General Ne Win, has transformed Burma. Despite a great wealth of natural resources, greedy and violent generals have followed a relentless path of deconstruction leading from prosperous, self-sufficient nationhood to Burma's present status as one of the UN's designated poorest twenty countries.

In late 2006 basic commodity prices for rice, cooking oil and other necessities rose sharply. Then, on August 15, 2007, with no advance notice, the government cancelled fuel subsidies, and overnight gasoline and oil prices doubled at the pump, and natural gas, used extensively for fueling cars as well as for cooking rose by 500%. At that point public protest began.

The regime's immediate response was violent — beating and arresting demonstrators, zeroing in on well-known dissidents. On September 5th, several hundred monks in the city of Pakokku marched and chanted the *Metta Sutta* in solidarity with a suffering nation. Troops attacked, tying up and beating three monks. The next day, young monks briefly took several government officials hostage. In a widely read leaflet, the All-Burma Monks' Alliance demanded that the military apologize for their brutal actions against Pakokku's monks.

* * *

By early December the rains passed and an uneasy silence fell across Burma. Four of us flew into Yangon International Airport on December 4th as a witness delegation sponsored by Buddhist Peace Fellowship. We had come to see how it was in Burma — to listen to the stories of monks and laypeople; to convey the international Buddhist community's solidarity with the people of Burma; and to open lines of communication and support for future work. Our group included Phra Paisan Visalo, a Thai forest monk and founder of Thailand's Buddhika network for engaged Buddhism; Nupphanat Anuphongphat (a.k.a. Top), also from Buddhika; Jill Jameson, a human rights activist and trainer from Melbourne's BPF chapter in Australia; and myself from BPF's national office.

I've been involved with Burma since 1991 when I began working at BPF. That year I traveled with a delegation from the International Network of Engaged Buddhists to Manerplaw, the large opposition encampment on the Burmese side of the Moie River, across from Thailand. (A year later, Manerplaw was overrun by Burmese troops.) Over the years I visited the border areas numerous times, sleeping with monks in jungle monasteries, visiting refugee camps down long muddy roads, bringing food and medicine to clinics and schools. I've walked through the smoking ashes of settlements, sat with monks shivering from malaria in the midst of an April heat wave, and wept to see the swollen bellies of hungry children in Burma's ethnic areas. But now I was in Rangoon for the first time.

Phra Paisan, Top, and I taxied into Rangoon from the airport. Time seemed to have stopped here decades ago. Even in rush hour, traffic was light on badly potholed streets.

60s vintage cars spewed exhaust. Sidewalks were filled with people walking to work and commuters jammed themselves into ramshackle busses and trucks. Where streets would ordinarily be teeming with monks and nuns, the only monks I saw were novice schoolboys and bent old men with their umbrellas and bowls.

Our cab driver interrogated us. His questions led uncomfortably beyond ordinary curiosity — why have you come to Burma and how long will you stay, who do you know in Yangon? Our responses were carefully framed. We knew we would be watched everywhere, and that official scrutiny had begun the minute we stepped off the plane. This was confirmed when Jill flew in a few hours later and we met at our hotel. Her taxi driver took her through the same kind of questions. Then he remarked that three men had come on an earlier flight — an American, a Thai monk, and another Thai — and asked if she were connected with them. We could only wonder what other connections had already been made. It set all of us on edge.

Over the next week we met with Burmese activists, monks, teachers, students, orphans, diplomats, and ordinary people in streets, monasteries, homes, teashops, and restaurants. We visited monasteries, schools, and bustling markets. We woke up before dawn to circumambulate the Shwedagon pagoda as the sun kindled fire on its golden flanks. A cloud of fear encircled all. In people's smiles, fear seemed close to the surface. But wherever we went, people were anxious to talk, to tell their stories about the long, painful months just past. All we could do was listen, that simple and essential *dhamma* practice. Listening builds bridges. We heard tales of violence and loss. Yet there was a remarkable lightness, too — a laugh, a look, the touch of a hand cutting through the almost unbearable words and memories.

But fear is not simply imposed from the outside. Around the public temples, monks usually avoided engaging with us. We feared for the safety of friends who might be seen talking with westerners. We could see they were themselves worried.

An activist friend explained, "We have a saying. If you have died once, you know how much the coffin costs." The price of Burmese resistance is high: not just in blood, but in the arising of trauma manifesting as anger, mistrust, and depression. Aung San Suu Kyi writes in *Freedom From Fear*, "It is not power that corrupts but fear. Fear of losing power corrupts those who wield it and fear of the scourge of power corrupts those who are subject to it."

* * *

POLICE VAN: RANGOON, BURMA: DECEMBER 2007

Where are the monks? We asked this wherever we went, and now, years later, it is still my question. In late September and in the weeks that followed, Burmese security forces raided dozens of monasteries. They often came late at night, beating monks, tearing robes from their bodies, shooting some, stealing and destroying religious objects. An activist friend,

Stephen, said that intelligence agents scanned photographs and videos, looking for four categories of monks and nuns involved in the protests. These were implicated by the junta for watching the protests, for clapping, offering water, and for actually marching, with a range of punishments and prison terms for such actions. Stephen also told us that a college friend, an officer in the military, said that officers and soldiers under his command got drunk before they raided a monastery under orders to beat monks while questioning them.

According to the Assistance Association for Political Prisoners, in Rangoon alone more than fifty monasteries were raided. In most cases, resident monks either fled or were sent to their home villages. We noted that in Rangoon, although almost all the monks we met were in full support of the demonstrations, not one admitted marching or taking part. (We did meet a number of participants in Mae Sot several days later.) Some monks were forcibly disrobed, and those identified as leaders of the All-Burma Monks Alliance were arrested and tortured. Many remain in prison. According to the Burmese opposition blog "Vimutti," 348 monasteries in and around Rangoon had a population of 29,658 monks and novices. As of February 7, 2008, only 6391 could be accounted for in these monasteries. In the aftermath of the repression, we found many large monasteries empty and locked. Other centers had military vehicles and barbed wire blocking access. At one monastery we were told that all the local nuns had fled after the crackdown, and that local people missed their morning chanting. Each of the centers we were able to visit — and these were places ostensibly not involved in the demonstrations — had government security officers at the gate. One morning, while we gave out packages of noodles to five hundred young children at a desperately poor monastic orphanage, we learned that military intelligence agents had followed us in and questioned the young abbot about our presence. They left — evidently feeding children was not illegal that day! — but their very presence left the school staff badly shaken.

Buddhist monastic schools and orphanages play a key role in the educational system. In the Rangoon Division alone there are 162 monastic schools. Across Burma there are hundreds of thousands of orphans, children who have lost a parent or whose families cannot afford even the small expense of government schools. There are some fine monastic schools, but the ones we saw on the outskirts of Rangoon were disturbing places. Hundreds of young children had to make do with thin rice gruel, maybe mixed with a touch of fish paste. They had no textbooks, and writing materials were precious. Children learned by rote memorization. Dormitories — home to dozens of students per room — were crowded and dirty. We saw a health worker checking the children for scabies and ringworm, conditions that were almost universal. Malnutrition, overcrowding, and limited staff mean that children are neglected despite the teachers' and monks' best intentions. And, in fact, this school, which had previously been home to nearly forty monks, was now staffed by just four or five, the rest having fled in October. That was not unique to one temple, but common in monasteries across Burma. We asked the abbot where they had gone. He didn't know. Looking down, he said he did not know if he would hear from any of them again.

* * *

Leaving Burma, we flew back to Bangkok, and traveled by van to Mae Sot along the Thai-Burma border, where we heard there was a cluster of Burmese monks who had fled Burma for the relative safety of Thailand.

Mae Sot is deep in the mountains of Thailand, just across the Moie River from Myawaddy on the Burmese side. It is a kind of wild-western place of dusty streets and teeming markets full of cheap goods. Illegal Burmese refugees account for roughly 80,000 of the population of 100,000. Another 75,000 refugees live in three large makeshift camps set up by Thai authorities in the nearby hills, cut off from opportunities for work and liberty. Around Mae Sot's garbage dump a score of children comb through mounds of refuse daily, salvaging anything that might be sold or bartered for food. On the outskirts of town two hundred prison-like factories are staffed by these illegal workers, manufacturing clothing and other bargain items for the world market, working for half the Thai minimum wage of around $4.50/day. Most of these women and men are from the neighboring Karen state inside Burma, where effectively there is no work. They are grateful for any work at all, but working behind barbed wire for such wages is exploitation nonetheless.

Mae Sot is also home to an astonishing number of opposition groups — local, national, and international. Each has its particular mission and constituency, and it is often difficult for them to work together across ethnic and political lines.

Despite its proximity to Burma, and a *laissez faire* attitude toward these displaced Burmese — Thai businesses need their cheap labor — sources told us that only several hundred refugees have made the difficult journey from central Burma to the border, and of those, perhaps twenty or thirty monks. The number is hard to pin down.

Through contacts with the local National League for Democracy and other activist organizations we were invited to talk with monks from Rangoon, Mandalay, and Bago at several Mae Sot safe houses. The houses themselves were inconspicuous, but hardly safe. Like many of the offices and residences of Burmese activists, they were subject to random raids by Thai immigration officers, who line their own pockets with bribes and remind the Burmese of their undocumented vulnerability in Thailand. Dr. Cynthia Maung's Mae Tao Clinic, the main medical resource for Burmese migrants and refugees along the border, has been raided countless times. Since Thailand never signed the 1951 Refugee Convention, it has blocked the United Nations High Commission for Refugees from registering and screening new arrivals, who are constantly subject to deportation and exploitation.

Talking with monks over cups of tea, their sense of insecurity was the first matter of conversation. Many of them are living along with lay people, a highly unusual and uncomfortable situation for Burmese monastics. The Thai *sangha* does not welcome or include them in their temple life, and Burmese monks are not permitted to go on alms-rounds for food. Their red robes make them dangerously conspicuous to immigration police. Even the established Burmese-style temples in Mae Sot do not allow them in residence. Without UNHCR refugee status, without financial support, without the sustaining regimen of *dhamma* practice together, these monks have left the street battles of Burma and entered a twilight zone of displacement on the Thai border. They deserve much better than this.

Some of the eleven monks we met had been religious leaders in their communities. They had varying degrees of political awareness along with their advanced study of *suttas* and *abhidhamma*. Several had been to university before ordination, and were familiar with social theory. Some were activist monks. Ashin K, who had fled Burma in 2006 at the urging of his abbot, wore a tattooed portrait of Aung San Suu Kyi on his chest, just under his robes. Others monks seemed traumatized. They had followed their brothers and their conscience into the streets, but had not anticipated the risks. What they saw in September at the hands of the SPDC has left deep shadows on their minds. Each of them had to disrobe temporarily to escape from the cities, using false papers and disguise to make their way across Burma. Crossing the border to presumptive safety, a *sayadaw* in this group was arrested by Thai police, and friends had to pay a bribe of $80 to save him from threatened repatriation. Understandably, some monks have given up their robes, melting into the larger community of Burmese in Mae Sot.

* * *

There is no end to this story, but there are many beginnings. I believe the Burmese *sangha* will survive, because I believe that *dhamma* itself cannot be harmed. I have seen the courage of monks, nuns, and laypeople whose training is so thorough that, with or without robes, they were able to sustain their practice of mindfulness and *metta* in the depths of prison. Even torture was not able to break their practice. This is grace under pressure, Aung San Suu Kyi wrote, "grace which is renewed repeatedly in the face of harsh, unremitting pressure." In the months since our return I see fearlessness flowering in the Burmese *sangha*. Here are some brief examples.

• Clandestine members of the All-Burma Monks Alliance called on student monks to boycott the annual monastic examinations at the lecturing monasteries. Their statement urged monks and laypeople to continue with the nonviolent democracy movement and not to give up. Their call was supported by senior teachers at several teaching monasteries.

• A December 2007 news item from Democratic Voice for Burma radio reported that four monasteries in Pakokku had maintained the alms boycott, passing government officials' offerings of food to the poor.

> ...A group of government officials led by the Magwe division Peace and Development Council chairman and the minister of electrical energy visited the monasteries earlier this month to give offerings of rice to the monks. The monastery head monks accepted the donations but would not give blessings to the officials in return. "We accepted the rice donation because it is not appropriate to reject an offering, but then later we donated the rice to poor people in the neighborhood."

• In a new year's 2008 statement, The All-Burmese Monks Alliance called on the people of Burma to continue their struggle against the regime, but stressed the necessity of nonviolence. They urged monks to continue with their boycott of the Burmese regime, until all monks and political prisoners have been released. They said, "If the public and monks join forces, we can resolve all our problems."

• Later in January, U Gambira, a leading young monk in September's demonstrations — held and tortured by the junta since early November — was charged with violating the Unlawful Assembly Act, facing at least three years in prison. He has yet to have a public court appearance, and supporters fear for his health.

• The new International Burmese Monks Organization (Sasana Moli) has set up branches in fourteen countries — including the United States, Europe, Canada, Bangladesh, New Zealand, Australia, Taiwan, Singapore, Malaysia, Thailand, Sri Lanka and India — to respond to the Burmese junta's violent suppression of the *sangha*. Sasana Moli's patron, the 81 year old Sayadaw U Kovida spoke about the monks' actions and their alms boycott:

> I am convinced that Burma will get democracy very soon and that this boycott will end successfully. The monks inside Burma want to remind us time and again that the boycott is still on. It does not matter that they are having food forced on them. What's more important is to realize that in their minds the struggle is still on. If they have the courage and vision and continue the fight, with support of the world, then Burma will see the light in the near future.

* * *

If suffering is the first noble truth, the suffering of Burmese sisters and brothers is not separate from what I see as my life. As a matter of practice I turn towards that suffering. I hope we can do this together. But it is also true, as Thich Nhat Hanh says: suffering is not enough. The joy of connection, of relatedness, is also present, as is our debt of gratitude for Burmese teachers who have carried the *dhamma* to the west. Then there is the necessary activity of a *bodhisattva*, pointing the way for sentient beings to liberate ourselves from our own personal prisons and from places like Burma, where the whole of society is a prison. We offer material aid, *dhamma* teachings, and the reality of fearlessness itself. The work is endless. In return the monks and nuns of Burma offer us the possibility of a nation and a world that truly courses in liberation.

EXILED SAFFRON REVOLUTION MONKS:
MAE SOT, THAILAND — DECEMBER 2007

DALIT CHILDREN: KONDHANPUR, INDIA — MARCH 2010

AMBEDKAR'S CHILDREN: INDIAN BUDDHISM REBORN AMONG THE UNTOUCHABLES

With justice on our side, I do not see how we can lose our battle. The battle to me is a matter of joy...For ours is a battle not for wealth or for power. It is a battle for freedom. It is a battle for the reclamation of the human personality.
— Dr. B.R. Ambedkar, All-India Depressed Classes Conference, 1942

In the land of Shakyamuni a modern Buddhist revolution is taking place hidden in plain sight. These Indian Buddhists, the untouchable castes, among the poorest of the poor, go by various names: neo-Buddhists, Dalit Buddhists, Navayanists, Ambedkarites. But like so much in their lives, the names carry a subtle odor of condescension — that their kind of Buddhism is something less than real. This is a mistaken view. To my mind, the opposite is true. The Buddhism that Dr. B.R. Ambedkar brought to his own untouchable communities is precisely the practice of Buddha, Dharma, Sangha and, as he put it, of Liberty, Equality, and Fraternity — the expression of liberated beings, and the kernel of a liberated and casteless society. Today it is alive among millions in India. Tomorrow this may well become the largest community of practitioners on the planet.

In Mumbai's Bandra East slums, Pune's impoverished Dapodi neighborhood, in the children's hostels and schools of Nagpur one finds modest *viharas* — with a Buddha image and a photo or print of Dr. Ambedker adorned with garlands of fresh flowers — where people sing the basic Pali chants, sit in meditation, and hear the dharma. Even in the narrowest of circumstances, I could feel their joy in the dharma and hunger for deeper practice and understanding. Untouchables have taken to Buddhism because they can and must. The Buddha was clear. He said: I teach about suffering and the end of suffering. For those who suffer day by day, year by year, this message is hope itself.

JAI BHIM! — AMBEDKAR, THE UNTOUCHABLES, AND CONVERSION. It was midnight by the time my endless flight arrived in Mumbai. I cleared Indian customs and immigration, and retrieved my bag. Walking out of the terminal I felt the warm coastal breeze and caught the mingled scents of sea air, the ripeness of a huge city, and sharp fumes of jet fuel. Outside a rectangular barrier hundreds of shouting, gesturing drivers, friends, and family members scanned the departing passengers. Twenty-four hours awake, I was glad to see a sign with my name on it and made my way past two military officers guarding a gap in the barrier.

Two smiling young men took me to a quiet place and said: "Jai Bhim! Sir, welcome to India." One placed a garland over my head, the other offered a bright bouquet of flowers. They led me off to car and hotel.

"Jai Bhim!" is how Indian Buddhists greet each other. It means "Victory to Bhim" or to Dr. Bhimrao Ambedkar, the founder of their movement. Buddhism in modern India flows directly from the dedication and mission of Ambedkar. The 2001 census puts India's Buddhist population at 8,000,000, more than 90% from the Dalit or untouchable communities. (Scholars suggest the numbers of uncounted or undeclared Buddhists are in the range of 30,000,000.) These communities are distributed across the nation, with the largest concentration of Buddhists in the Indian state of Maharashtra. Buddhist identity is rooted in Indian history, but it had to be reclaimed with a political and social assertion of freedom led by a remarkable figure — Dr. B.R. Ambedkar — less than sixty years ago.

Bhimrao Ramji Ambedkar (or Babasaheb as his devotees call him) was born in 1891 to a poor but educated Mahar family. Traditionally the Mahars — the largest untouchable caste in Maharashtra — lived outside the boundaries of a village and worked as servants, watchmen, street-sweepers, and haulers of animal carcasses. Dr. Ambedkar's father served in the colonial Indian Army. By virtue of his brilliance and good fortune the young Ambedkar was among the first untouchables to attend an Indian university, and by his early thirties he had earned doctorates from Columbia University, the London School of Economics, and a place at the bar at London's Gray's Inn. He came back as one of the best-educated men in India. Yet returning from England to work in Baroda he was unable to find housing, and barred from dining with his colleagues. He suffered the indignity of clerks tossing files on his desk for fear of his "polluting" touch.

The "hell of caste" that Ambedkar experienced in his youth is hard for many of us in the west to imagine despite our own history of racism. Caste means hereditary bondage passed from generation to generation under a dominant Brahmanic or Hindu social reality. Contrary to the Buddhist meaning of these same words, in this system *karma* means fate or the caste one is born into, and *dharma* means the duty to live out one's life within the confines of caste responsibilities. This duty includes strict endogamy, or marriage only within one's caste.

The many untouchable or Dalit communities, differentiated by region, ethnicity and (sub)caste have been identified with butchering, removal of rubbish, sweeping, removal of human waste and dead animals, leatherwork, and so on. Such occupations are still seen as impure activities, polluting to higher castes. And that pollution is somehow contagious. As impure, untouchables were excluded from aspects of ordinary Hindu life. They were not allowed to enter temples, go to schools, or even to live within the boundaries of rural villages. Though untouchability was legally abolished by India's secular constitution of 1950, the reality is not much improved today.

Hillary Maxwell, in a June 2003 edition of "National Geographic News," wrote:

> Human rights abuses against these people, known as Dalits, are legion. A random sampling of headlines in mainstream Indian newspapers tells their story: "Dalit boy beaten to death for plucking flowers;" "Dalit tortured by cops for three days;" "Dalit 'witch' paraded naked in Bihar;" "Dalit killed in lock-up at Kurnool;" "7 Dalits burnt alive in caste clash;" "5 Dalits lynched in Haryana;" "Dalit woman gang-raped, paraded naked;" "Police egged on mob to lynch Dalits."

Maxwell adds:

India's Untouchables are relegated to the lowest jobs, and live in constant fear of being publicly humiliated, paraded naked, beaten, and raped with impunity by upper-caste Hindus seeking to keep them in their place. Merely walking through an upper-caste neighborhood is a life-threatening offense.

Dr. Ambedkar came up with this name for untouchables: "Dalit," meaning people who are "broken to pieces" or suppressed. Other names have been suggested, each problematic, seen as demeaning by one group or another: Scheduled Castes and Scheduled Tribes (roughly 300,000,000 or 25% of India's population) are the sanitized terms used in the Indian constitution; untouchable is a legally proscribed status; ex-untouchable is euphemism. Gandhi's term *harijan*, which means "children of god," is patronizing to adults who hardly feel themselves blessed by any divine presence.

These are the harsh realities Dr. Ambedkar faced in the 1920s and 30s. While Gandhi was forging a nonviolent anti-colonial movement, Ambedkar — who often clashed with Gandhi — worked for human rights and the annihilation of caste as essential to what many saw as an otherwise elite-driven nationalism. After years of attempted collaboration with reformist Hindus, including Gandhi, Ambedkar, a member of the Bombay legislature and a leader of the Mahar conference, organized a 1927 *satyagraha* (meaning, roughly, "truth-force") of thousands to draw water and drink from the Chowdar Tank, a reservoir closed to untouchables despite a 1923 resolution of the Bombay Council. That same year, Ambedkar took a radical symbolic step of publicly burning the *Manusmrti,* the Brahmanic code of caste duty, which he and other Dalit leaders saw as key to the social, economic, religious, and political oppression of the untouchables.

By 1935 Dr. Ambedkar concluded that the dominant Brahmin/Hindu caste system could not be reformed even with support from most liberal-minded Hindus. Caste oppression was not an artifact of Brahmanism but its essence. Ambedkar urged the untouchables to give up the idea of attaining Hindu religious rights. He prepared to leave Hinduism and adopt another religion. He saw caste as a "system of graded inequality," in which each sub-caste measures itself above some castes and below others, creating an almost infinite factionalism, dividing each exploited community against another, making unity of social or political purpose almost impossible. Ambedkar said: "I was born a Hindu, but I solemnly assure you that I will not die as a Hindu." For years he investigated Islam, Christianity, and Sikhism — and was courted by each of these groups, who were well aware that Ambedkar's conversion would bring along millions of untouchables and the promise of wide political power.

In the late 1940s Ambedkar decided that Buddhism was the logical home for his people, as indigenous to India, where it had been the defining religious tradition for nearly 1500 years. He wrote:

> The teachings of Buddha are eternal, but even then Buddha did not proclaim them to be infallible. The religion of Buddha has the capacity to change according to times, a quality which no other religion can claim to have...Now what is the basis of Buddhism? If you study carefully, you will see that Buddhism is based on reason. There is an element of flexibility inherent in it, which is not found in any other religion.

But plans for conversion were postponed while Dr. Ambedkar served as India's first law minister and leader of the constitutional drafting committee. In the early 1950s, setting aside his political career, he plunged into the study of Buddhism and its application to the shaping of a new Dalit identity. After long consideration and consultation, and in ill health, feeling the shadow of mortality, Dr. Ambedkar converted on October 14, 1956 at the Deekshabhoomi (Conversion Ground) in Nagpur, taking the Three Refuges in Buddha, Dharma, Sangha, and receiving the *pancasila* or five ethical precepts from the senior Buddhist monk in India, U Chandramani. Then he did an unprecedented thing, particularly unprecedented for a layperson. Turning to 400,000 followers who were present, he offered them the three refuges and his own twenty-two vows, which included the five precepts and the renunciation of specific articles of Hindu practice and belief. This signaled a momentous renewal of Buddhism in India. A number of mass conversions followed within weeks. But by early December, less than two months later, Dr. Ambedkar died from complications of diabetes and heart disease.

THE NEW BUDDHIST MOVEMENT AND TBMSG

Despite the conversion of millions of Dalits, Dr. Ambedkar's death left the spiritual and political movement of untouchables without unified leadership. Politically it was not surprising to see the rapid rise of factionalism among the Dalits, given that entrenched system of graded inequality. No one else on the scene had his intellect and strength of character with which to unify the many outcast communities. Mangesh Dahiwale of the Manuski Center says:

> People looked at Dr. Babasaheb Ambedkar as a kind of guide or guru or philosopher who would lead them after conversion. *The Buddha and His Dhamma* was published a year after Dr. Ambedkar's death and it became a source that people turned towards to understand Buddhism. It was published in English first, and then soon translated into Marathi and Hindi. That book was a guide, and people began to read it and study it in study groups.

In Ambedkar's day there were virtually no Buddhist teachers in India, but, as Mangesh explains:

> Naturally people flocked around the Sri Lankan and Burmese Buddhists, anyone who could offer Buddhist teachings. If they found a bhikkhu, they would gather around and try to understand what Buddhism is. In fact some of the people from the Ambedkarite movement, in the 1950s, became monks in India, ordained in a Sri Lankan tradition.

Today the painful fact is that Buddhists in Asian and Western dharma circles have paid scant attention to the Ambedkarite Buddhists. Like the oppression of caste, their needs and realities are almost invisible to those outside the circle of oppression. But the process Dr. Ambedkar set in motion was incomplete. From 1956 until the early 1980s there was little continuing education or practice available to millions who converted. But the right seeds had been planted. According to Mangesh Dahiwale:

> Babasaheb Ambedkar had created the Bhartiya Bauddha Mahasabha or the Buddhist Society of India in 1955. The first mass conversions were held under their auspices. But for the most part these were local initiatives, because people were acting locally. The start of this movement was grassroots and Indian led. Really there were no teachers or prominent leaders, because ordinary people took the initiative. Even though Dr. Ambedkar was not there, his inspiration was there. People tried to do what they could. Mainly they were very poor, facing discrimination, but they tried to keep the flame alive.

This network of local viharas and practitioners, scattered across Maharastra and other parts of India, allowed young English monk, Ven. Sangharakshita, to connect with the Dalit Buddhist movement. Sangharakshita was strongly called to Dr. Ambedkar and his work with the Dalits. Before Ambedkar's death they had an opportunity to meet several times, and by chance Sangharakshita was in Nagpur the evening Ambedkar passed away in Delhi, and was asked to speak at a meeting of condolence. He writes:

> By the time I rose to speak — standing on the seat of a rickshaw, and with someone holding a microphone in front of me — about 100,000 people had gathered. By rights I should have been the last speaker but as things turned out I was the first. In fact I was the only speaker. Not that there were not others who wanted to pay tribute to the memory of the departed leader. One by one, some five or six of Ambedkar's most prominent local supporters attempted to speak, and one by one they were forced to sit down again as, overcome by emotion, they burst into tears after uttering only a few words.

From this moment Sangharakshita's sense of personal responsibility was clear.

> During the decade that followed I spent much of my time with the ex-untouchable Buddhists of Nagpur, Bombay, Poona, Jabalpur, and Ahmedabad, as well as with those who lived in the small towns and villages of central and western India. I learned to admire their cheerfulness, their friendliness, their intelligence, and their loyalty to the memory of their great emancipator.

Returning to Great Britain, where he founded the Friends of the Western Buddhist Order (FWBO), Sangharakshita kept thinking about the Dalit Buddhists and his friends in India. He encouraged a young disciple, Lokamitra, to visit India and think about working with the Ambedkarite Buddhists.

Dhammachari Lokamitra is a tall, solid, and youthful-looking Englishman with an easy laugh and a quick mind. His energy at 62 hints at a kind of wildness tempered by years of dharma practice. Lokamitra lives with his family in a modest house in the Ambedkar Colony settlement of Pune. Since 1978, he has helped to build a movement, Trailokya Bauddha Mahasangha Sahayaka Gana (TBMSG), the Indian wing of FWBO, and a variety of related social organizations, all which aimed to develop a new Indian or Ambedkarite Buddhism, fusing dharma practice and social action.

Lokamitra came to India in 1977 to study yoga in Pune with B.S. Iyengar. Breaking the long train trip from Calcutta in Nagpur, by chance he arrived on the 21st anniversary of Dr. Ambedkar's conversion. As an FWBO *angarika,* wearing robes, he found himself on a large stage at the Deekshabhoomi, facing thousands of Ambedkar's devotees.

> In the 36 hours we spent in Nagpur I entered a new world, a world of millions of the most oppressed people, all desperate to transform their lives and their society through Buddhism, but with little living teaching to guide them. I had stumbled blindly into a situation in which the two-fold transformation seemed a real possibility, and on the most auspicious of days. I did not consciously decide to live and work in India then but I have no doubt that my future was decided on that day.

Lokamitra moved to India the following year, and with help of local Indian Buddhists organized retreats and meditation groups. He says, "Our friends organized these where they could, a disused railway carriage, the veranda of an unfinished police station, a small garage when its car went to church on Sundays."

More than thirty years have passed since those rough and ready days. TBMSG now includes five hundred Indian order members and many thousands of practitioners. With the support of Karuna Trust and other donors in Asia and the west, two related organizations — Bahujan Hitay (meaning "for the welfare of many") and Jambudvipa Trust have evolved to do outreach and social work among the Dalits. More recently they have created the Manuski Project — where I stayed in Pune — with leadership from my friends Maitreyanath Dhammakirti, Mangesh Dahiwale, and Priyadarshi Telang (among others). Manuski is the Marathi word Dr. Ambedkar used for "humanity" or "humanness." The center's mission is:

1. Transcending caste barriers through Social Development Program
2. Fighting social discrimination through legal and constitutional ways
3. Developing Dalit women leadership
4. Sustainability of the social projects and building solidarity amongst the individuals and organizations

The network of related organizations, like Indra's net, comprises retreat centers, hostels, adult education, atrocity and civil rights work, earthquake and tsunami relief, school programs and more in Maharashtra, Uttar Pradesh, Gujurat, Tamil Nadu, Andhra Pradesh.

GLIMPSES OF LIBERATION

I must apologize for some sweeping generalizations. Two weeks in India, my first time there, goes by quickly. I saw just a little of the astonishing richness, diversity, and contradictions of this country. But my experience was wonderful and very powerful — the sweetness, sincerity, intelligence, and generosity of those I met stay with me. A piece of my heart remains with friends in Maharashtra.

Walking out of the Mumbai airport, just looking out the car window at busy night streets, I formed first impressions of India that lasted to the journey's end. Having spent time elsewhere in south Asia — Burma, Bangladesh, and Sri Lanka — where war and civil strife prevail — I sensed a freedom and intimacy among people in India, even in the midst of jarring discrepancies of wealth and standing. It felt strangely familiar to me, and familial in the best (and maybe in the worst) sense of the word. There is something to the fact that India is the world's largest democracy. Democracy there is every bit as flawed as it is in the U.S., but the energy of people in the streets and fields is limitless.

Kaleidoscopic impressions could fill many pages; instead I would like to convey a sense of the heartfelt Buddhist practice I encountered. The point of my journey was simply to be with people, to teach and to learn from them. My friend Mangesh and his comrades kept me busy from the moment I arrived in Pune until my last talk in Mumbai and the late night flight home.

Manuski is "Action Central" for Dalit social work. The center itself is quiet and cool, with a good library, meeting rooms, offices, a number of basic but comfortable guest rooms, and a large meditation hall. After a visit to the Dapodi slum projects and a long briefing on TBMSG and its network, in the evening I was scheduled to give a dharma talk. There were about forty people for meditation and lecture, most of them neatly dressed men in their thirties, and about six or eight women. Speaking after meditation, mindful that everything had to be translated into Marathi, I tried to keep my words simple. I spoke about the Soto Zen principle of "practice realization," that we don't sit to *attain* enlightenment, but because we are *already* enlightened. I folded in teachings from Suzuki Roshi — "you yourself are Buddha." My hope was simply to be encouraging, addressing an audience that was still wrestling daily with the wounds of caste.

From the start, in talks and meetings, I wanted to support free inquiry and gender equality. These are points which Dr. Ambedkar identified as the essence of Buddhism. I left time for question and answer at each meeting, which was something of a novelty. Students and practitioners were more used to receiving teachings, hesitant to question. Second, I openly invited equal participation from women in all discussions. It was not always possible to be completely evenhanded. Some women need encouragement to step outside a circle of silence, to speak out and question. Women now lead many of the social projects, and there are more than ninety women teachers or *dhamma-charinis* in TBMSG. But the movement still needs to have more women in visible leadership, which means participating equally in public events and internal organizational structures. In order to arrive at equality, men, and particularly men in leadership, have to step back and be allies for the women.

Over the next two weeks, I gave workshops on engaged Buddhism, met with students at Nagaloka, took part in a study retreat in Kondhanpur, and offered dharma talks in Nagpur and Mumbai. Each activity included melodic Pali chanting and meditation. The strong feeling in a meditation hall cannot be faked. One can sense a quality of concentration and settledness in people's bodies and expressions, from the subtle (or un-subtle) adjustments of posture. It is clear just from the respectful way people dress. In California people tend to be pretty casual, but for meditation or a dharma talk in India it is customary to wear attractive and functional clothes. Men come in slacks and loose or business shirts. Women wear bright saris, which suggest shared origins with the robes of monks and nuns. The meditation practices of TBMSG are straightforward and familiar to me: *anapanasati* or mindfulness of breathing and *metta bhavana*/cultivation of lovingkindness.

We made a day-trip to two of India's oldest rock-cut Buddhist caves. Bhaja is a 200 BCE hillside cave complex across a green Deccan valley from TBMSG's Sadhamma Pradeep retreat center. The caves were quiet and still, with the shadows of morning falling across its ancient monks' quarters and simple carvings. Close by, the Karla caves have been co-opted by local Hindus who have set up a temple at the cave entrance, where at festival time priests sacrifice the goats and chickens devotees bring as offerings. Since we happened to go on Holi, the Hindu festival of colors, sacrifices were in full swing. When our car died of vapor lock, I got a ride up the narrow hillside with four young men on their way to the temple, one of whom cradled a chicken for sacrifice. Unlike the serenity of the Bhaja, the steep winding stairs at Karla were lined with snack and souvenir vendors hawking their wares and with beggars of every age and infirmity. The hillside itself was strewn with trash — papers, plastic bags and bottles, food scraps — in stark contrast to the fine clothes and happy mood of the Hindu families coming for the holiday.

NAGALOKA

Nagaloka or the Nagarjuna Training Institute (NTI) is TBMSG's flagship educational project, the largest of its centers. NTI has a 15-acre campus on the outskirts of Nagpur, where Dr. Ambedkar converted to Buddhism, at the geographical center of India. At night, from a distance, one can see the tall golden image of a walking Buddha that smiles down on the students of Nagaloka.

NTI offers a ten-month leadership training in basic Buddhism and social action. This program, working with Dalit young people from all religious communities, has graduated almost five hundred young people from twenty Indian states over the last eight years. Most of these students have gone back to their villages to work on campaigns against social oppression, offer dharma, and support other young people to live and train in Nagpur. For many students leaving home for the first time is unsettling and difficult. Each young woman and man comes from a particular region and village with a common yearning to see the world and to be of use. But growing up within oppressive traditional cultures leaves them unprepared for the culture shock of a new life at Nagaloka. Some of these young people are overwhelmed, but most find their way into student life, buoyed up by new friends and teachers, and by the practice of dhamma.

Caste-based village life is marked by discrimination and violence. Even as I write, CNN reports the murder of an Indian politician in Uttar Pradesh, shot down as he attended a ceremony marking B.R. Ambedkar's birth. Students at Nagaloka have grown up with such violence. I tried to bring out their stories, so I could learn about them and so they could learn from each other. One young man recounted:

> In my childhood I observed this caste system all the time. My grandmother had to take water from the village well. But when she put her bucket in, other community people saw that and would not take water until the well was purified by rituals. If someone asked you to their home for food, if you were Dalit, you had to wash your own plate. My father often used to do that. Once I was invited for dinner, but I refused to wash my plate. They asked why I wouldn't wash it. I said, if you invite me to eat with you, it is not right to force me to wash my own plate. In that case, I can give up your food and go. So I just left.

A woman of twenty said:

> I am from Orissa. Where I live there is still a very strong caste system. They don't allow Dalit children to get any kind of education. If

a girl tries to get an education, their parents become afraid and get them married quickly. Neighborhood people will not allow the girls to learn as they wish to. We are here at Nagaloka now, but my family doesn't know we are learning Buddhism. When we go back to the village we will share them what we have learned about the dharma. We came with the help of former students, and when we go back we will help find other students. I really believe that our training at Nagloka will benefit our community.

The school explains its mission this way:

The different Scheduled caste communities in India do not usually cooperate with each other, even after they have become Buddhists. At the Nagarjuna Institute they relate to each other just as Buddhists and not in terms of the caste they have come from. This in itself is an enormous contribution to a truly democratic society. The intensive practice for a year with other Buddhists from all over India means they cease to identify with the old untouchable caste but just as Buddhists.

I was inspired by the students at Nagaloka. Meeting them over several days, hours a day, their stories touched me. Their way-seeking minds glow with the spirit of inquiry. Having been in the fields of engaged Buddhism for twenty years, nowhere else have I met young people with their kind of intuitive grasp of Buddhism and social action arising together. Nowhere else have I had deeper discussion that never slipped into abstraction, but focused on the conditions of oppression these students know too well. Nowhere have I encountered anything like their determination to remake the world in peace. My heart is with them.

LIBERTY, EQUALITY, FRATERNITY
In an All-India Radio broadcast two years before his conversion, Dr. Ambedkar said:

> Positively, my social philosophy may be said to be enshrined in three words: liberty, equality, and fraternity. Let no one however say that I have borrowed my philosophy from the French Revolution. I have not. My philosophy has its roots in religion and not in political science. I have derived them from the teachings of my master, the Buddha.

After the 1956 conversion he raised up another ideal — Buddha, Dharma, Sangha. One morning in my bed on our retreat at Kondhanpur, I realized that these two ideals are in fact one. At the moment it seemed like an original insight. But when I mentioned it to Lokamitra he laughed, saying this had been a central point of discussions about Ambedkarite Buddhism in the early 80s.

Liberty is the quality of actualized liberation as embodied by the Buddha. But as in the realization of enlightened life, liberty is a practice, something that must be aspired to and worked at. It is not a static quality.

Equality is dharma in the sense that we see all beings as equal. Zen Master Hakuin's "Song of Buddhism" says: "From the beginning all beings are Buddha." Each sentient being is precious. All people are chosen — not just those of a particular religion, caste, or nation. At the same time, Dr. Ambedkar understood that each person has strengths and weaknesses, skills and shortcomings. In this respect we are unequal and individual, unique. But taken together, liberty and equality encourage us to be completely ourselves, as large and open as possible, respecting and valuing each other as precious.

Fraternity is the cutting edge of Ambedkar's Buddhism and the new Buddhist movement. Fraternity is sangha, the community of practitioners, and the wider community of all beings (hence, linked to equality). In the Buddha's time there was a "fourfold sangha:" monks, nuns, laymen, laywomen. Somehow Asian Buddhism has reduced this to the onefold sangha — monks. This is not the idea of Buddhism Dr. Ambedkar had.

Fraternity is a challenge for the Dalit community. It challenges them just as race, class, and diversity challenge western Buddhists. The social realities of India draw clear lines between all the religions — Hindu, Muslim, Sikh, Christian, and Buddhist; between caste and non-caste peoples; and, most critically, among the many Dalit groups themselves within the system of "graded inequality," each group scrambling for the tiniest privileges of social position, economic opportunity, and political power. Fraternity is what connects us. And we know this is hard work.

There is much in this new Indian Buddhism that we share in the west. On both sides we have turned to the dharma in response to the Buddha's central message about suffering and its end. Knowingly or not, many of us in the West come to Buddhism to deal with suffering, often alienated from religious traditions we were born to. For Dalits, whose material circumstances may be so different from ours, the motivation is the same: to learn about suffering and to reach its end, in each person's life and in society.

What I call the "three marks" of Western Buddhism are shared by Ambedkarites. Theirs is a largely a "lay" Buddhist movement, comprising family members, workers, and lay teachers, much like our own centers here in America. Dr. Ambedkar was highly critical of Asia's monastic orders, which he saw as elitist and uninterested in establishing Buddhist practice for laypeople. So it is not surprising that the new Buddhists have created a lay or lay-ordained movement. The model of TBMSG/FWBO is an order of *dhammacharis/ dhammacharinis* — meaning followers of the dharma. Order members are meditation teachers, study leaders, and ministers. As Suzuki Roshi said about his own students: You are not quite priest, not quite lay.

The second mark is feminization. Dr. Ambedkar said: "I measure the progress of a community by the degree of progress which women have achieved." Women's progress is evident in urban India. In rural areas, though, patriarchal culture is tenacious, closely linked to caste and Hindu *dharma*. But among the Ambedkarites, in slums and poor villages, Buddhist women are leading schools, hostels, social work, and dharma communities as teachers or *dharmacharinis* in their own right.

The third mark is social action, or the unity of dharma practice and social work — compassion in action. When I came to work at Buddhist Peace Fellowship in 1991, engaged Buddhism was outside the mainstream. Twenty years later, countless centers and groups are involved in prison work, chaplaincy, feeding the poor, and organizing against war. We have come to see this as a responsibility that flows from the bodhisattva vow to save all beings. But from the start, Dr. Ambedkar's vision of Buddhism incorporated a vision of society and social liberation, far beyond the introspective caricature that some have of Buddhism. So it is natural that an Indian Buddhism movement, rooted in the most oppressed, would see the oneness of personal development and social transformation.

With all this in common, it is painful that Indian Buddhism is almost invisible to Buddhists around the world. I could speculate on why this is so, but simply said, the time has come for us to see that a vast engaged movement in India promises to change the way Buddhism is seen by all the world's religions.

Ambedkarite Buddhists hunger for dharma and for contact with the wider world. Very few from outside FWBO go to

India to practice with TBMSG and other Buddhists. It is not that the Dalits need Buddhist "missionaries." Native Indian teachers are well-trained in the Buddha's teachings. But they need our help, resources, and they need to be seen and valued in the world. And as the dharma rises in the slums and in the poorest villages across India, we can learn, be inspired, and rededicate ourselves to liberation for all beings, irrespective of class, caste, gender, and tribe.

LEAVING MUMBAI
Without seeing, listening to, and smelling them, India's slums are beyond imagination. The sprawling shantytowns of *Slumdog Millionaire* (or the South African shacks of Neill Blomkamp's *District 9*) are not fantasy. They are real and pervasive, growing like weeds just behind the main roads and shops of every Indian city. They surround and threaten wealthy high-rises. Obscene affluence and obscene poverty battle for a future in which each is creating the other.

Speaking of Pune, India's eighth largest city, 40% Dalit slum-dwellers, my friend Maitreyanath said:

> In Pune, for example there are around 850 slums, nearly 600 of them are "authorized slums." These slums are "holding banks" for local political leaders. They try to persuade the government to give services to the slums, so people will get benefit, and political leaders can say we brought you water, roads, and so on. Then they get the votes from these authorized slums. That is the way the system works.

Mumbai is like Pune on steroids. Nearly fifteen million people, 55% of them in the slums. (There is an excellent book about it: *Maximum City* by Suketu Mehta.) The slums of Mumbai and other cities are cobbled together of corrugated metal, sheets of plastic, and scraps of wood. They rise at the most unlikely angles, leaning together over alleyways no more than three or four feet wide, where one finds children playing, young men huddled over cards, women washing clothes, scrawny dogs, chickens and goats picking through trash piles and puddles of excrement. At the center of the city shacks rise two or three stories, with the same makeshift construction and scavenged materials. It is amazing to see these structures at night, leaning against each other, with candles or oil lamps or bare electric bulbs shining through windowless portals.

Running water is often a spigot down the block. Toilets are a quiet corner behind a building, an abandoned lot, or a reeking communal structure with three or four stalls and no plumbing. Electricity is stolen with a makeshift cable spliced into a mainline.

But life is everywhere tenacious. Joy and self-respect spring up in unlikely places. Slum children see me coming blocks away. They laugh and tease the bald, big-nose stranger. Though their houses may be falling around them, women and men take care to go out in clean clothes.

Maharashtra is the population center of Dalit Buddhists. In the poorest neighborhoods, along with storefront temples and mosques, it is common to find a Buddhist *vihara*. A plastic tarp or corrugated roof covers an open square surrounded by shanties. A white or golden Buddha, adorned with fresh flowers, with a garlanded image of Babasaheb Ambedkar sits within a small wooden enclosure. Worn carpets are rolled out so men can sit on one side, women on the other. City sounds rise within the silence of meditation — children's shouts, panting rickshaws, barking dogs, the crack of a cricket bat, a street vendor's cry. The peace of meditation at once includes all of this and goes beyond it.

Life is unfolding. Here and everywhere, enlightenment is unfolding in the simple, common human activity of sitting down. Half a world away from home, I feel completely at home. The ordinariness is amazing: sitting with friends in the middle of this urban jungle.

After thirty minutes a bell rings. I take a drink from my water bottle and begin to speak. My words are unplanned, but mysteriously they take shape, just as this wonderful community has taken shape, arriving one by one in the dust and bustle of their lives. My message is that practice is not some special activity, separate from the ordinary things of life. Dharma pervades all that we do. The Buddhas are here with us in the cool glow of evening. Dr. Ambedkar is here, too. In just this moment — which cannot be captured or defiled — freedom is at hand.

Select Bibliography:
• *The Buddha and His Dharma*, B.R. Ambedkar: Re-published for free distribution by The Corporate Body of the Buddha Educational Foundation, Taiwan <www.budaedu.org/en/book/II-02main.php3>
• *The Essential Writings of B.R. Ambedkar*, V Rodrigues (ed), Delhi: Oxford University Press, 2002.
• *Ambedkar and Buddhism*, Sangharakshita, Glasgow: Windhorse, 1986.
• *Jai Bhim — Dispatches from a Peaceful Revolution*, Terry Pilchik (Nagabodhi), Glasgow: Windhorse, 2004.
• *Dr. Ambedkar and Untouchability*, Christophe Jaffrelot; Delhi: Paul's Press, 2005.

Links:
www.tbmsg.org/
www.clearviewproject.org
www.nagaloka.org/
www.manuski.org/
www.navayan.com

STUDENTS AT NAGARJUNA TRAINING INSTITUTE:
NAGPUR, INDIA — MARCH 2010

BROKEN SHIPS: CHITTAGONG, BANGLADESH — 2000

SHIPBREAKING

...but have a care how you seize the privilege of Jonah alone; the privilege of discoursing upon the joists and beams; the rafters, ridge-pole, sleepers, and under-pinnings, making up the frame-work of leviathan...
—Herman Melville, *Moby Dick*

The great ships come to die on a narrow beach outside Chittagong, in the southeast of Bangladesh on the Bay of Bengal. The beach extends gradually into the murky green water, then drops off steeply into the Bay. In Singapore a captain has been hired on to command a skeleton crew for this last voyage. Near Chittagong, at high tide, he hands the helm to a Bangladeshi pilot who knows the local waters. The ship's new owner paces the bridge behind the captain and pilot. Tired old diesel engines power up as fast as the engineer dares and the vessel lurches toward the shore. The pilot must know just where he is going. From far offshore, running at full throttle, he has to arrive at a slot of beach no more than a hundred yards wide. So the owner is understandably nervous. The ship accelerates steadily into the shallows. There is a jolt, a deep groan and grinding, the end of all forward motion as the ship drives onto the muddy shore. The big engines shut down for good.

At low tide men come with drills and hammers and torches, the basic tools of their trade. Nothing more sophisticated is used. They hole the hull below the waterline and the old ship will move no more, except in bits and pieces that find their way into factories and homes all across Bangladesh. The coast guard comes on board and removes navigation equipment, radios, and any weapons the vessel may carry as protection against pirates, numerous in many parts of the world. Then ship cutters go right to work on the massive hull, wasting no time marking out their plan of attack.

Crews of laborers, wiry energetic men, wade out to the ship and begin to dismantle and carry away equipment, tools, wiring, furniture, fittings, everyday items of modern life. A ship at sea carries all this with her. She is a floating village. When the work is done there are not even bones left. Every piece of that ship is measured and sold; every thing in that ship is put to use.

Native peoples hunting for whales practice the same total economy. Each part of the animal, flesh and bone, has a use. The big old ships rest in the mud like beached whales, gutted and stripped. Thick sludge oozes from bilges and tanks like spoiled blood. In time, towering sections of rusty steel that remain create a crazy geometry on the shore, until they themselves are cut into small pieces and carried off to a rerolling mill.

Under a winter sun I stand on the beach near these vast ships. In the distance, long lines of men haul thick cables out to the hulls mired in shallow water and mud. At the MAK shipbreaking yard only a stern section with big engines remains in the water. The rest has been picked apart. The ship is gone. But south of us dozens of ships stand in rank for more than five miles, each in its own particular state of deconstruction. A large cross section of another ship is burning in the adjacent yard. Thick black smoke and orange flames rise from residual sludge in the hull that has somehow caught fire. A carelessly directed cutting torch, or a match. No effort is being made to put it out. There is no fire extinguishing equipment in sight. The cutters just work around it.

How I Got Here

In the summer of 1996 I was studying Zen Buddhism with Robert Aitken in Hawaii. Aitken Roshi recommended an exhibition of photographs at the Honolulu Academy of Art, "Workers," by the Brazilian photographer Sebastiao Salgado. I was stunned by Salgado's intensely dramatic and compassionate work, his love and perplexity for the poorest and most disempowered people. Salgado's photographs of shipbreaking in Bangladesh particularly spoke to me. I wanted to walk among these ships and talk with the men who worked there.

I got close the following winter, when I led a witness delegation to Bangladesh's Chittagong Hill Tracts, home to a small minority of tribal Buddhists in a sea of Bengali Muslims. *(See an addendum at the end of this essay, a column I wrote about the Chittagong Hill Tracts in a 1998 issue of "Turning Wheel.")*

Shipbreaking evokes a meditation on the fine points of interdependence in a modern world. Shakyamuni Buddha taught: Because there is this, there is that. Nothing stands by itself. So what is the link, the strong symbiosis between these wiry-bodied Bangladeshi men, their families, and those of us living in relative comfort half a world away? What is my responsibility to these people, and theirs to me? What about the great ships, masterworks of industrial technology, built at vast expense, and sold for scrap? Each year twenty-seven thousand ocean-going vessels carry oil, automobiles, and consumer goods around the world. Five billion tons of cargo. The things they carry are essential to both to our lives and our illusions of well-being. But what about the lives and dreams of the shipbreakers themselves? In the midst of their strenuous and dangerous work, what are their hopes, their illusions?

Shipbreaking

Shipbreaking thrives in the world's peripheral vision at the margin of the global economy. This is a new industry in South Asia. Until the 1970s, shipbreaking was still a highly mechanized process done at shipyards and dry docks in the West. It was hard, honorable work, not badly paid. Cranes and winches did the heavy lifting. But rising labor costs, shrinking markets for scrap and nautical goods, and increasing awareness about hazardous waste and occupational safety meant that shipbreaking's future was not in the West.

By the late 1980s, ninety percent of the cutting was being done in India, Pakistan, and Bangladesh. Labor is cheap and plentiful there; concern about hazardous waste is minimal, and occupational safety regulations are nonexistent. A large ship contains several tons of asbestos, liquid PCBs used for electrical insulation, lead, organo-tin and mercury-based paints, and petroleum sludge. In the vast shipbreaking yards of Alang in India there is a funeral a day. Ghats where the bodies burn are right there on the beach, right by the corpses of ships.

Shipbreaking in Bangladesh began in 1960 when a ship beached in a cyclone couldn't be refloated. The owners simply sold the stranded vessel to new owners who cut it up on the spot. In 1970 there was another cyclone and two more ships ran aground. During the brutal liberation war between Bangladesh and Pakistan in 1971, the fledgling Bangladesh airforce issued an international alert prohibiting shipping to Chittagong. Ships which ignored the warnings were sunk then scrapped.

By 1978 there were enough workers, contractors, and vendors for an integrated industry to take shape. Steel from shipbreaking is the basic stuff of Bangladeshi industry. Scrap steel is cut up into sheets, loaded on a truck and weighed on big scales. It is sold to a local buyer who resells to a local steel-rolling mill where it is chopped, melted, and hot rolled into construction materials. A million tons a year. These mills are often small operations: twenty or thirty men, forges, milling machines, and lathes. Images of the early industrial revolution. The remaining contents of the ship are sold to dealers in Chittagong and Dhaka. Not a part is wasted.

WORKERS

Depending on the size of the ship — oil tankers, container ships, and cargo vessels — two hundred or more men and boys hire on for the duration of the breaking. Laborers, cutters, fitters, supervisors. The starting pay for laborers is 60 Taka or about $1.25 for eight hours. It goes up depending on experience and skill. The days are long — from seven or eight in the morning until dark — so there is plenty of overtime. Most of the workers are of an age with the ships themselves, twenty-five to thirty years. They come from the rural north of Bangladesh, agricultural districts owned by absentee landlords or higher caste village headmen. They own no lands themselves, and back home there is no work to sustain them and their families. Hard as the shipbreaking work may be, they are glad to have a job. If they want to stay on, there is always another ship.

The laborers are mostly dark-skinned young men. It's a man's world, as is much of Muslim Bangladesh. In other manual trades — road building, construction, brick making — low-caste women do the grunt work, but not in shipbreaking. The men are barefoot, wearing cheap cotton *lungyis* tied at the waist. With a shout, fifteen or twenty of them lift a thick steel plate carved from the hull. The group leader jumps up for a ride on this makeshift platform. He leads a rhythmic song as they carry the steel up the beach to a loading zone. A supervisor follows along, in spotless western clothes with an umbrella, keeping up a brisk pace. When several crews are at work, their chanting makes a strange modern-sounding music, punctuated by loud sounds of hammers on metal. Men and women have always lightened their work with song. Their smiles and grimaces are genuine, not contrived for my camera.

Workers take their meals and tea breaks close by. The owners have built a dormitory right on site and most of the men live there rent free. The men themselves hire an experienced cook. He and a helper prepare filling meals of rice, lentils, curried vegetables, and sometimes a small portion of fish or meat, in big blackened pots over open fires. Shipbreakers pay a premium for their meals, sixty cents a day, which is nearly half the daily wage for some.

MOHAMMED, YOUNG WORKER: CHITTAGONG,
BANGLADESH — 2000

• The boy in grimy clothes, gloves in hand, stands in front of a concrete wall. This wall represents his future. Mohammed is twelve, though he looks younger. He has been following us around the yard with a quizzical smile, but now he is uneasy having his picture taken and answering questions. Mohammed lives nearby, in a small village near the highway. He has a mother, father, sister, and two older brothers. His twenty-year-old brother works in this same yard.

Mohammed's job, which he shares with several other boys, is to comb the grounds for small scraps, nuts and bolts, which are collected and melted down by the nearby mills. He works barefoot, like almost all the other laborers, with a tall red bucket on his shoulder. He has only been working here for a month, earning considerably less than the older workers. He takes home 200 Taka per week, about $4, which he gives to his mother.

He comes to work in clean clothes every morning, and changes to worn work clothes. At noon he changes back and goes home for lunch. Then he returns to the yard for the rest of the afternoon. He no longer goes to school, but can read haltingly. Mohammed's eyes challenge me.

• Abdul Samad is a cutter, age twenty-six. He stands with a confident, easy grace. When he smiles, I can see red betel nut stains on his teeth and gums. Abdul began as a helper, but for a year and a half he has been making good wages for his skill with a cutting torch. He stays at a rented house, a mile from the yard.

He is not married; his parents live in the north. It's a poor farming area, and there is almost no work to be had. Abdul says if God wishes, he can do better at shipbreaking than working the land. He explains that he likes his job, but even if he didn't like it, he has nothing else to do for wages. So he writes letters to his parents and goes home every few months, getting leave from the foreman if he is working on a ship.

Abdul works from eight in the morning until dark. He supplies his own clothing and gear — which is marked by many scorch marks — gloves, shoes, and goggles. He has no hardhat.

OWNERS
Abul Kashem is the co-owner of MAK Corporation, in partnership with a cousin. Both men are in their middle forties. We met on a Friday, the traditional day of worship for Muslims. They wore woven skullcaps and long elegant white shirts, *thobe*. The cousins were mistrustful at first, worried that I was an American journalist, an environmentalist, or a government agent (which government?). It took a while to assure them that I was just interested in seeing the ships and the men, and coming to understand how things work. Kashem was kind enough to respond, "If your objective of study is beneficial for the total trade and business of shipbreaking in Bangladesh, then of course I will help." I nodded my assent, though even my objective was not quite so neutral. But Master Kashem welcomed us back several times over the next few days, talked at length over tea, and allowed us to wander freely through the MAK yard.

Master Kashem purchased the *MV Kallang* for scrap, 3939 tons, in Singapore from Electra Maritime, Jersey, Great Britain. What's left of the ship lies strewn across his yard. Kashem enjoyed the *Kallang's* last short voyage, making sure the pilot knew just where to come aground. The *Kallang*, which sailed under various flags as *Pioneer, Tropeoferos,* and *Wistaria Purple*, was built in Singapore in 1974. This is the usual life span of an oceangoing ship. After twenty or thirty years of constant motion and salt water, paint won't cover the tired, rusting metal. When the original term of insurance expires, most ships go for scrap.

It will take three or four months to cut and carry away this ship. When I visit they are well into the process. The *Kallang's* prow lies askew in the mud. The stern, with her bridge and heavy turbines still in place, rests several hundred yards further out in shallow waters.

Kallang is Master Kashem's first vessel, but he has been around the scrap business for years, trading electrical goods and furniture from a shop in the city. "I learned all about this trade. Now when somebody comes to purchase goods from us, I know what to sell, whom to sell to, how much I should charge. I know the inside of this trade, so those traders cannot cheat me." Because of his business experience the banks were willing to help with the purchase, lending some $361,000, plus import tax, duty, and local tax — a lot of money in Bangladesh.

Owners take a purely financial gamble. Master Kashem bought the *Kallang* for $92 a ton. Within a year's time the price of scrap has fluctuated between $60 and $170 per ton, depending on the availability and the spot price of steel on the world market. By the time cutting is complete, prices may be drastically different. The cost of yard space on the beach has gone from $2000 to $20,000 in a handful of years. Shipbreakers who have lost their gamble have a tendency to disappear with whatever cash remains, leaving Bangladeshi banks holding bad loans. So banks are understandably reluctant to lend money. In this period of financial crisis all across Asia, the bankers get up to thirty percent return on loans to shipbreakers. So men like Master Kashem and his cousin have to know their trade. You can see his confidence in the way he talks and holds his body. But confidence is not always enough. "Inshallah" or "God willing" is his watchword.

VENDORS

Chittagong is the second city of Bangladesh, at the mouth of the Karnapuli River, which flows out of the Chittagong Hill Tracts to the east. It has always been a seaport and a center for commerce. Centuries ago it was key to the spice trades between Europe and Asia. A modern garment industry serving the West flourishes here today.

Along the highway north of Chittagong, vendors in cluttered shops sell everything imaginable from off the ships. Each shop specializes in one particular kind of goods. I saw turbines, generators, pumps, machine tools, electrical fixtures, wiring, stoves, refrigerators, cooking pots, plates, knives, forks, spoons, beds, furniture, navigational charts and guides, books, videotapes, and medical supplies.

Huge motors and generators look almost organic in their complexity. They are coated with grease and grime, rusty and corroded. Yet there is a market for such things. Like many poor people Bangladeshis have learned to be good with their hands. They have a knack for keeping things running as long as they can.

Shops in Chittagong city and Dhaka sell silverware and plates with shipping companies' insignia. Nautical furniture, made of materials that resist warping and swelling in damp environments, are ideal for a country like Bangladesh, with its long rainy season and periodic flooding.

THOUGHTS

Wasteland shapes of broken ships on the beach at Chittagong demark the frontier of industrial society. The scene recalls distant planets in the Star Wars movies: technology and decay and dust all mixed together in wide vistas. Crossections of ships lie embedded in the mud. Staircases and passageways lead to nowhere at odd angles. Huge funnels look lost and alone, toppled off their high perch.

Bearing witness to the human dimension of shipbreaking— thin young men old before their time, but still proud and energetic — I see a touching, redemptive quality to the work itself. (The workers probably have very different thoughts about redemption!) Men put their hearts and backs into it. They sing as they carry thick plates of steel. These labors save them, even temporarily, from a bleak future of agrarian emptiness.

This gets to the heart of my concern. Oceangoing vessels carrying consumer goods around the world are essential to the quality of life we have in America. Like all things, ships live and die. When their time comes to die, ship owners send them to remote corners of Asia, far from our sight. In the West we tend to hide the things that make us uncomfortable. But there is much to learn from our discomforts.

South Asia needs the work. It's true. This is one side. According to the World Bank, nearly one billion people in Asia live on less than $1 per day. And the cheap scrap materials will be well used there. This is the last word in recycling. There are no mines in Bangladesh, no manufacture of heavy equipment, so shipbreaking is a valuable resource.

On the other side, a large ship contains tons of toxic materials. In a village just beyond the MAK yard, children play around a holding tank for used oil. On the coast road one evening I saw a tank truck spilling sludge on the highway, laying down a steady stream. Two vehicles coming along behind skidded across the oily road, and a large truck carrying heavy machinery overturned on the soft shoulder.

The Basel Action Network (BAN) and Greenpeace have been calling for implementation of the 1995 Basel Convention on the control and disposal of hazardous wastes, signed by more than a hundred nations (not including the United States). Under this convention, the export of scrap ships laden with toxic substances from members of the Organization of Economic Cooperation and Development (OECD) — the twenty-nine most wealthy and industrialized countries — to poor countries like Bangladesh is prohibited. Ships must be purged of contaminants before they are sold. In practice this is rarely done. In a 1998 critique of the U.S. Interagency Panel on Ship Scrapping, BAN wrote that, "a mandate to sell ships is not a license to kill. It is not a mandate to sell them without regard to health and safety of human beings." Principles of environmental justice mean that society's most hazardous enterprises must not be located disproportionately in poor communities and nations.

By the year 2010, nearly sixty-eight million shipping tons will come onto the global scrap market. Despite the Basel Convention, it is likely that most of these sixty-eight million tons will be sold as is, hazardous waste and toxins along for the ride to distant destinations.

WE SHOULD KNOW HOW IT COMES TO US... AND WHERE IT GOES

At the Zen center where I live we recite a verse before eating: "Innumerable labors brought us this food. We should know how it comes to us." Understanding innumerable labors is my vow. Like most vows, it can't ever be kept completely. Knowing how things come to us also implies knowing where things go. Where does our garbage go? Our junked cars? The chemical residue of our industries? The great ships that cross and re-cross our oceans? And what is life like for the people who handle such things?

The men who break ships in Bangladesh are just working — to support themselves and their families. They accept this work, gratefully or not. But a complicated chain of conditions offers them one kind of life in a poor country like Bangladesh, and offers me a very different life in the bosom of the empire. Buddhists may call this karma. Muslims might say it is God's will. But either way the truth is complex.

Karma simply means action, which calls forth result. In a world of action and result, denial is no refuge. If my eyes are open I can see that the labors of shipbreakers, the labors of poor people around the world are not freely offered. Not to us. Foremen, supervisors, bosses, corporations, ultimately you and I compel them. This is a kind of theft hiding behind the lies that we think of as economics or politics as usual.

How we live together on this planet, how we struggle to balance the inequalities of life — Bangladesh and America raising stark contrasts — makes a difference. It will continue to make a difference to our children, and their children — if we haven't used up our world by then. If shipbreaking is work we all depend on, can we see past ourselves, and look at each other eye to eye?

* * *

ADDENDUM: REPORT FROM THE CHITTAGONG HILL TRACTS, 1998

The road into the Chittagong Hill Tracts, in southeastern Bangladesh, winds up from the port city of Chittagong on the Bay of Bengal, past a long strand where huge ships are beached and broken down for scrap. It passes through teeming bazaars full of bone-thin men and endless blocks of shabby apartments. It meanders through flat green paddy land, where Bengali farmers scrape out a bare living, up into the rolling hills, with their stripped-out forests, enticing valleys, and ubiquitous army encampments and checkpoints.

Not much traffic as you climb the narrow, pockmarked road into the Chittagong Hill Tracts towards Khagrachari, one of the few large towns in this remote region. The only vehicles are buses with passengers spilling onto the roof, a few baby taxis spewing dark, oily exhaust as they labor up the steep incline, and military vehicles full of impeccably uniformed Bengali soldiers.

I've been back from Bangladesh for three months, and the images and memories still come to me in a flood. As they stream along, I have a hard time knowing just what to share with you, and I wonder about my personal responsibility, as I recall bitter realities and painful, impoverished lives.

I spent two weeks in Bangladesh this March — traveling, witnessing, and working with INEB's Ordained Sangha: socially engaged monks, nuns, priests and ordained people of different religious traditions. The center of my long journey was the Ordained Sangha meeting at Parbatya Bouddha Mission, a spacious rural temple and orphans' school in the Chittagong Hill Tracts. For seven years, the abbot, my friend

Ven. Sumanalankar, has been inviting me to visit him in Kha-grachari. Only recently was the Bangladesh government willing to let us in.

After 20 years of guerrilla war, there is a moment to breathe in the Chittagong Hill Tracts. This once-forested region has been home to 600,000 tribal people for several centuries — mostly Chakma and Marma Buddhists, Tripura Hindus, and many animist groups, in contrast to more than 120 million Bengali Muslims who live in the alluvial plains to the west. In 1900 British colonizers recognized the fragile balance of populations and set regulations that limited the migration and settlement of Bengali Muslims in the Hill Tracts. But with the partition of India and Pakistan in 1947, and the brutal war for Bangladesh independence in 1971, the CHT was once again vulnerable to settlement by a rapidly expanding Bengali population, and also vulnerable to outside exploitation of its forests, lands, and minerals.

In the late 1950s and early '60s, the government created a huge lake and hydroelectric plant at Kaptai in the Hill Tracts, which flooded rich valleys and destroyed 40 percent of the arable land. One hundred thousand hill people were displaced without compensation, and many fled to India. The ancient tradition of swidden agriculture, called jhum, was no longer practical. Too much land had been destroyed. More land was lost in the years after independence as the Bangladesh government implemented a policy of Bengali settlement in the hills. This set the stage for 20 years of forced relocation, murder, torture, cultural oppression, and fierce rebellion. It has been a bitter civil war, unseen and unheeded by most of the world.

In December 1997, a peace accord was signed by the government, the military, the hill people's political organization (the Jana Sanghati Samity or JSS), and its armed wing, the Shanti Bahini. The day before we arrived in the Hill Tracts, several thousand insurgents had surrendered weapons in a ceremony at the sports arena in Khagrachari. It was the second such ceremony, and it expressed an intention of peace, if not the realization of justice. The challenge now is implementation: resettling and compensating exiled hill people, building schools and indigenous institutions, developing democracy, and healing wounds of war. Can this be accomplished in the face of pervasive poverty, unchecked population growth, and global systems of exploitation? We must try.

This is an old commitment for Buddhist Peace Fellowship, our first international program, in fact. Board member Michael Roche traveled to the Hill Tracts in 1980 and wrote a series of reports for BPF and IFOR. We undertook political lobbying with the U.S. Congress and began to send money to orphanages in Bangladesh. Long friendship with the Chakma monk Bimal Bhikkhu, still exiled in Calcutta, has kept our contact fresh even though foreigners were banned from the CHT for many years. But monks, organizers, and church groups knew we were watching. Over and over as I traveled, hill people expressed gratitude for BPF's attention and support. It is important to them to be heard by people from the outside world.

The short time I spent in Bangladesh was not easy. With my friends Ven. Bodhinyana and Sister Cecilia, a Catholic nun, I traveled to the cities of Chittagong, Cox's Bazaar, and Teknaf, far from the capital of Dhaka. I saw burned-out homes of poor Hindus, desecrated stupas, a rickshaw driver collapsed by the roadside, and officious military police at checkpoints in the CHT. In the streets, young mothers held out their frail babies and beseeched us for alms.

But I also met curious, friendly, generous people of many ethnicities. From the bus window, I could see Bengali men walking arm in arm, coming home from the fields in early evening. In Dhaka and Rangamati we visited Banophool and Moanaghar, two large schools and orphanages housing hundreds of children from the CHT. They are partly financed by Partage, a French organization founded by Thich Nhat Hanh's student Pierre Marchand, who personally took on his teacher's message to save the world's children.

Distilling needs is a slow process. From discussions at the Ordained Sangha meeting and long talks with Santikaro Bhikkhu, Brother Jarlath D'Souza, Ven. Sumanalankar, Ven. Bodhinyana, and others, we are evolving a long-range plan so that monks in the Hill Tracts can help their own people. This plan — jointly undertaken by BPF, INEB, and BPF-Bangladesh — calls for dhamma education, meditation instruction, critical thinking, non-violence training, and reconciliation work. It calls for great patience, and we all wonder whether we can act in time.

As night falls, the children at Parbatya Bouddha Mission chant their lessons in dimly-lit dormitories. From their separate spaces, girls' and boys' voices mingle in nearby fields. The sweet, musical sound contrasts with the violence they have all witnessed. How close to the surface the violence is, even in myself. How vulnerable these children are. In Bangladesh I could also see the illusion we have in the West that our own vulnerability is protected, buried beneath layers of self and possession. When we stand with these children, with the hill people, we set aside all separation and allow our true vulnerability to arise. The Chittagong Hill Tracts are very close. I wish I could show you more.

— Berkeley, 2000

SHIPBREAKING WORKERS:
CHITTAGONG, BANGLADESH — 2000

NOTES TO GOD: WESTERN WALL, JERUSALEM — 2001

THROUGH A GLASS, DARKLY: A BUDDHIST PERSPECTIVE ON ISRAEL & PALESTINE

Each time I speak about the conflict in Israel and Palestine I seem to get it wrong. And silence will not do either. This is what Zen Buddhist practitioners call a *koan*. The challenge of a *koan* is to embody and present one's truth in a way that is neither self-centered nor dualistic, even in the face of ambiguity. No *koan* could be more urgent than the mutual destruction we are called on to witness daily in the Holy Land.

An old Chinese Buddhist verse says, "If you create an understanding of holiness, you will succumb to all errors." Our Buddhist understanding is that all the world is a holy land, and all the people in it. I and all beings include each other. Elevating one place, one people, or one practice as holy splits the world and plants seeds of "us and them." From such seeds war and hatred grow. The soil of the Holy Land has run with blood countless times in the name of what is holy. Holiness can be a cover for hatred and hunger for power. Great volumes of blood have been spilled, hardening our hearts rather than sanctifying them. So we ask ourselves what truly is the holy life?

In his First Letter to the Corinthians, Paul writes: "For now we see as through a glass, darkly." And Paul himself can hardly be seen as the font of tolerance. As a Buddhist, born a Jew, I tend to accept wisdom from all available spiritual sources. Our limited view, our self-centered attachment to views is the root of suffering. Self-centeredness causes us to live at the expense of others. That becomes a kind of cultural or national self-centeredness, with individual suffering manifesting as distorted policies. People and nations find ourselves out of harmony with the Buddha's first grave precept and the Bible's sixth commandment — do not kill. We pray that our brother and sister Israelis and Palestinians will widen their views and forsake violence in all forms — military, paramilitary, and suicide bombing. Violent reaction is not surprising from people scarred by greed, hatred, and delusion, who then create national entities poisoned by these hungers and fears. Buddhist social analyst David Loy suggests we see this conflict

> "...not as a holy war between good and evil, but as a tragic cycle of reciprocal violence and hatred fuelled by a vicious cycle of escalating fear on both sides. Israelis fear that they will never be able to live at peace, believing that Palestinians are determined to destroy them. Palestinians, impoverished by Israeli control over their own communities and dominated by its U.S.-supplied military, strike back in the only way they can."

An apocalyptic myth has taken hold in Israel/Palestine. It promises mutual destruction and threatens to set the whole world on fire. My friend Eve Marko, a Zen teacher with roots in Israel, writes, "Conventional rational presentations won't do the trick. This is where spiritually-based activism can really contribute — with a different vision of human possibilities."

As Buddhists here in the United States, we need first to understand how our own vision is clouded. The U.S. media is distorted, compromised by its own corporate interests and its complicity with the U.S. government. We will have to look elsewhere — to independent and European press for good information about daily events and about the lives of ordinary Palestinians and Israelis.

We can try to put ourselves in the place of Israelis and Palestinians. Even though it is an impossible task, we must try to imagine ourselves living in their conditions. It seems we are so many miles away, and yet our lives and the fate of Israelis and Palestinians are connected, in ways that go beyond violence, armed struggle, and the oxymoronic "War on Terrorism."

In Buddhist practice we try to understand the subtle workings of cause and effect — karma and its fruits. When one sees the workings of karma, the natural response is one of repentance, vow, and renewal. The Mahayana liturgy of repentance goes like this.

> All my ancient twisted karma
> From beginningless greed, hatred, and delusion
> Born of body, speech, and mind,
> I now fully avow

We can trace these troubles back across the walls of time. Ishmael and Isaac, and their mothers Hagar and Sarah, vied for the affections of the patriarch Abraham. Greeks and Romans occupied Jerusalem and Palestine at the apex of their empires. Palestine was the elusive prize sought in bloody Crusades that served as a crucible for European and Islamic identities. A succession of empires — Ottoman, British, French, and others — ruled with a heavy hand, suppressing local cultures and playing them off against each other. And yet there is also a history of Jews and Muslims living as neighbors, in harmony. Conflict is not the only flavor. Then we come to the last six decades, an age of Holocaust, ethnic hatred, oil politics, and neo-colonialism.

The Buddhist principle of karma is rooted in beginningless greed, hatred, and delusion. The notion of social or national karma and fruit, cause and effect, is controversial, not the least because it is often used to blame victims for their own oppression. My investigation of karma begins at home. Though we cannot see all the causes that create our own lives, we try to see each strand of action, what we as Americans have created, inherited, and continue to create.

In our own memory and in the memory of our parents, the U.S. turned away potential European victims of the Nazi holocaust, sending them back to perish. Allied Forces failed to bomb railroad tracks leading to the death camps. These were anti-Semitic acts rooted in the systemic anti-Semitism of American society and politics, policies that put little value on Jewish lives. U.S. support for the creation of Israel at the expense of indigenous Palestinians, who were uprooted from their land in 1948, then again in 1967, was motivated not by kindness, but by politics that were an extension of these same anti-Semitic policies. Anti-Semitism is not simply anti-Jewishness. Many in the Middle East have a Semitic root, traced back to Shem, the son of Noah. International politics have turned two peoples of one Semitic root against each other. Our continuing support, helping Israel to build the region's dominant military force, has also created a client state for the implementation of U.S. policy.

There are surely people of good will on the American diplomatic team, but I fear the United States is compromised historically and too self-interested to play the leading role in peacemaking or keeping. Although the U.S. bills itself as the one remaining superpower, our leaders fail to understand that economic and military power is not equivalent to moral authority. In fact, power tends to undermine such authority in even the most principled men and women. Only when our government can openly acknowledge its complicity with violence and stop pouring arms into the region will it have the moral authority to convince rather than coerce others.

The history above is, of course, highly condensed and short on nuance. The effect of such history is to create a mind of victimization. Every side can point to ancient and recent wounds as justification for present acts. This is much like the dynamic of an abusive family, where wounds are nurtured and transmitted from generation to generation, forging chains of suffering out of fear and anger. Verses 3-5 of the *Dhammapada* speak to this.

> He insulted me, hit me, beat me, robbed me
> — for those who brood on this, hostility isn't stilled.
> He insulted me, hit me, beat me, robbed me
> — for those who don't brood on this, hostility is stilled.
> Hostilities are not stilled through hostilities, regardless.
> Hostilities are stilled through non-hostility:
> This, an unending truth.

I offer this perspective as no more than a partial truth. But I encourage you to do your own investigation of history and karma. Each of us must take responsibility for our actions and those done by our nation in our name. We take up the age-old practice of repentance and renewal, and learn not to see ourselves as victims.

* * *

We see through a glass, darkly, but there are rays of hope. They shine apart from the flash of bombs and the flare of burning homes. Many ordinary and extraordinary people in Israel and Palestine, and in Europe and the U.S., believe in the work of inner disarmament, bringing their faith and courage forward for the sake of peace. This work — begun in the quiet space of introspection — is very hard. It means setting aside our sense of righteousness and the notion of "my" pain that must be avenged blow for blow.

• Each Friday for 18 months now, a small group of Israelis and Palestinians, Jews, Muslims, and Christians have been meeting in a narrow Jerusalem courtyard overlooking the Western Wall and Al-Aqsa mosque. They sit in a circle, practicing peace. Before them is the Temple Mount and the great mosques. Around them are young women and men of the Israeli border police, tough but not entirely unfriendly, and on guard, with their automatic rifles at ready. I sat in this circle among friends last year, when the Intifada was intensifying. It was astonishing to be so close to the conflict, so close to holy places, literally surrounded by weapons. Our vigil seemed at once ordinary, powerful, and not enough. One wishes this circle might magically grow and link hands around all of Jerusalem. Eliyahu McLean writes: "In a time when many in our circle feel deeply challenged to do something positive, silence and shared prayer seems to be the most powerful contributions we can offer at this most unforgiving time."

• More than four hundred thirty Israeli Army "refuseniks" (www.couragetorefuse.org) have vowed not to continue to serve in the occupation. Forty of them have been imprisoned. Their petition reads in part:

> "...We, combat officers and soldiers who have served the State of Israel for long weeks every year, in spite of the dear cost to our personal lives, have been on reserve duty all over the Occupied Territories, and were issued commands and directives that had nothing to do with the security of our country, and that had the sole purpose of perpetuating our control over the Palestinian people. We, whose eyes have seen the bloody toll this Occupation exacts from both sides. We, who sensed how the commands issued to us in the Territories, destroy all the values we had absorbed while growing up in this country. We, who understand now that the price of Occupation is the loss of IDF's (Israeli Defense Force's) human

character and the corruption of the entire Israeli society. We, who know that the Territories are not Israel, and that all settlements are bound to be evacuated in the end.

"We hereby declare that we shall not continue to fight this War of the Settlements. We shall not continue to fight beyond the 1967 borders in order to dominate, expel, starve and humiliate an entire people. We hereby declare that we shall continue serving in the Israel Defense Forces in any mission that serves Israel's defense. The missions of occupation and oppression do not serve this purpose, and we shall take no part in them."

• In the spring of 2002 at least forty peace activists — French, German, Italian, Canadian, American, as well as Israeli and Palestinian — walked into Yassir Arafat's compound while it was under siege. They remained there until he was freed, bearing witness, protecting life, risking their lives for the sake of peace. Other nonviolent activists have quietly taken up residence in the principal towns of the West Bank and in Jenin, Aida, and Al-Azza, besieged Palestinian Refugee Camps.

• In the U.S., Women in Black and Communities in Black regularly sit in silent witness to the destruction and loss of life on both sides. This loose-knit network of nonviolent activists <www.womeninblack.net> was started in Israel in 1988 by women seeking peace between Israel and Palestine and an end to Israeli occupation of the West Bank and Gaza. It also has roots in groups such as Mothers of the Disappeared in Argentina, Black Sash in South Africa, and the Women in Black movements in the former Yugoslavia. This movement has become worldwide, including women and families caught in many wars and conflicts. In their mission statement Women in Black write:

"Our silence is visible. We invite women to stand with us, reflect about themselves and women who have been raped, tortured or killed in concentration camps, women who have disappeared, whose loved ones have disappeared or have been killed, whose homes have been demolished. We wear black as a symbol to mourn for all victims of war, to mourn the destruction of people, nature and the fabric of life."

These are a few models for bearing witness and healing. They are not *the* solution to the Israeli-Palestinian conflict. Solutions are varied and difficult to enact, and we must find our own way, with a willingness to make mistakes. We must speak to our leaders and say what we think. We can engage in dialogue with Muslim and Jewish friends, keeping heart and mind open to all points of view, seeing the particular sufferings that move us all.

There are numerous obstacles and approaches to peace. We study, talk, and argue about peace until the small hours of many nights. I am willing to say that I believe in a two-state solution that recognizes autonomous states of Israel and Palestine within the pre-1967 boundaries, with nonviolent protocols for the resolution of political, economic, and religious conflicts. But it is really those two peoples themselves who must find their own path to peace and justice. I hope that the peoples of the region can find a way to communicate directly and leave their duplicitous and demagogic leaders behind them. These leaders — Netanyahu and Abbas at this point in time — have done little more than bring death and grief to each other's people and ultimately to themselves. My heart sinks each time I see them posturing for the cameras.

Recent demonstrations in San Francisco and Washington are also a ray of hope. These events were large, diverse, and expressive of complex understandings of the Middle East situation and U.S. policy. After so many months of media propaganda that offers nothing but support for George Bush's "war on terrorism," it was refreshing to see so many people, including Palestinians, Jews, African Americans, anti-globalization activists, and more, able to show publicly that there are other points of view. While we may not agree with all these perspectives, and we question the usefulness of positions that advocate meeting violence with violence, just to see families, working people, and youth in the streets is a good sign.

We must go beyond that, as international peace activists have done when they protect life and place themselves in harm's way. This kind of activity is the work of Bodhisattvas practicing "identity-action," enacting the principle that each of us is our brother's brother and our sister's sister. Again, Eve Marko writes:

> "...another step needs to be taken. We need to face those faceless tanks and feel what it's like when that turret moves around to point at you, all its guns aimed right at you. At that moment you don't remember that they shouldn't be shooting at Americans or at journalists — they did — all you can think of are those guns pointed right at you, that life has come to this. Till peacemakers are ready to stand in that place, in the place where soldiers stand, feel their fear and panic, I don't believe that peacemaking will have the trust, respect, and legitimacy needed to be really effective. We'll be seen as playing things too safe, without coming up with real alternatives to violence."

* * *

Whatever we do as Buddhist activists should be infused with generosity — *dana paramita*. When we address our own political leaders and those in the Middle East, we should do so with respect for their human strengths, understanding their frailties, and hoping for their innate wisdom. Even when we speak strongly to them, we practice generosity, as we would to ourselves. The practice of generosity has three aspects: giving material goods, truth, and fearlessness. With these principles in mind, we can begin to see how to help ordinary people near and far.

* * *

We seek peace and justice for Israel and Palestine. We return to our *koan*. Conventionally, peace is understood as the cessation of armed violence. Conventionally, justice is identified with punishment. Such an understanding of peace and justice pulls in two directions. The peace and justice we speak of here is *one* thing, *one* direction. As I said earlier, it is simply not living at the expense of another. It might, in fact, mean laying down one's life for another.

"For now we see as through a glass, darkly." As long as we live in this suffering world we must try to see each other. Take away the glass itself and look at your brother or sister eye to eye. We can do this in silence, without words or actions. When we sit this way, face to face, it is very difficult to depersonalize our opponent, to reduce him or her to a bitter rhetorical flourish. There is simply no way to avoid the clear fact of our shared humanity. By virtue of causes and conditions, past wounds and present fear, there will always be people who will not accept peace. Dogen Zenji wrote, "The mind of a sentient being is difficult to change." Still we practice to be the peace we envision. This is Buddha's peace and God's peace. This is something we can do, irrespective of Sharon, Arafat, Bush, and others. This may be our most precious offering. From there we can proceed to words and actions.

— *Autumn, 2002*

POSTSCRIPT

In the years since I wrote this piece nothing has gotten any better. If anything, positions have hardened and new fractures have appeared. Hamas won an election victory over Fatah, the other main Palestinian party, in January of 2006. Despite findings by international observers that the election was fair, the US and the European Union rejected the election results, and continue to label Hamas a terrorist organization. A year later, in June of 2007, Hamas and Fatah themselves waged a fierce battle for control of Gaza, the most densely-populated area of Palestine. Hamas victory in Gaza led to an escalation of rocket attacks on nearby Israel.

Predictably, Israel responded with an almost-total blockade of supplies to Gaza, then a military attack on the Strip in March of 2008.

Most recently, May of 2010, international activists organized a flotilla to supply Gaza with basic medical and food supplies. The six ships of the Gaza Freedom Flotilla were boarded and seized by Israeli commandos in international waters on the Mediterranean Sea. On board the Turkish *MV Mahi Mamara*, nine international activists were killed and dozens wounded, including seven Israeli commandos. International investigation into these attacks has just begun. As I write, new aid flotillas are being organized to break the Gaza blockade.

Conditions in the Palestinian West Bank, also under Israeli military control, are not much better. Since 2002 Israel has been building a high wall, planned to snake 436 miles through the territory, separating Palestinian and Israeli villages and population centers. There is still no moratorium on the building of Israeli settlements on what is nominally Palestinian territory. Nor is there any real end to military and paramilitary attacks from either side, though the preponderance of deaths and casualties falls on Palestinian communities.

The glass is ever darker. Hope is in short supply. Yet people on both sides yearn for peace and an end to violence. For this to happen, soldiers and politicians, ideologues of every stripe will have to set aside their beliefs. Men on both sides lay claim to freedom and righteousness, and go after it with missiles, bombs, and guns. If, as Lear says, "Nothing will come of nothing," how much less will come from the madness of war without end?

— June 2010

WALKING IN THE DIRECTION OF BEAUTY: SPEAKING WITH SISTER CHAN KHONG

— **Interviewed by Susan Moon and Alan Senauke in 1993**

Sister Chan Khong ("True Emptiness") is a Vietnamese nun who works closely with Thich Nhat Hanh, and lives in the community of Plum Village in Southern France. Sister Chan Khong, formerly known as Cao Ngoc Phuong, was well known as a Buddhist activist during the Vietnam War. She came to Paris to work with Thich Nhat Hanh and the Buddhist Peace Delegation, trying to influence the Paris Peace Talks. Though living in exile from Vietnam, she runs a program of aid to the poor in Vietnam (through a network of Buddhist social workers inside the country).

In the fall of 1993 she was on a teaching tour in the U.S. with Thich Nhat Hanh. Susan Moon and Alan Senauke talked with her at Kim Son Monastery in Watsonville, California. We sat together in a grove of cypress trees overlooking the ocean, while gray-robed monks and nuns passed quietly back and forth around us, making preparations for a retreat.

* * *

Susan Moon: The amount of suffering that you've seen and worked with is great. One can never do enough, there is always more work to do. And sometimes you even fail at a task: for example, tragically, some boat people you are trying to help end up getting drowned. How do you deal with despair in your work?

Sister Chan Khong: It is a matter of survival. Everyone is capable of serenity when nothing difficult is before them. But when there are bombs dropping, you can be overcome by fear and hatred. When our friends were murdered doing social service in Vietnam, we did our best to calm ourselves. We saw that in order to survive we had to walk in the direction of beauty. We were not yet able to love those who murdered our friends, but should we take guns? If we kill the murderer, how about his wife; his wife will be angry at us. And then his son will be angry at us.

When our friends were killed, the last thing their murderers said to them was, "I'm sorry but I have to kill you." We cannot thank those who killed our friends, but we can try to find some good small seed in them.

In the eulogy read at our friends' funeral, we spoke to the murderers: "Thank you for saying 'I am sorry.' We understand that there were pressures and threats on you and if you disobeyed the order to kill our friends, you could have been killed yourselves." After that eulogy, none of our social workers were attacked.

When thousands of boat people were adrift on the high seas, I was filled with despair. I completely identified myself with their suffering, and after many months of meditation, I initiated a rescue project. I rented a fishing boat in Thailand, dressed up like a fisherman, and went out to sea to "fish" out the boat people. Meditation allowed me to transform the garbage, the suffering, in me into a mercy fishing boat. On the seas, I was fearless, even when faced by pirates, and I was even joyful because I knew I was going in the direction of beauty.

SM: What about when it's not a crisis situation? Do you ever feel that you just don't have enough strength or patience to keep going on?

CK: When my close friends died, I suffered a lot. But I kept on reciting the "Heart Sutra": ...no birth, no death, no increasing, no decreasing...all day long. When I'm discouraged, it helps me a lot.

SM: How has being a woman affected your work and your practice?

CK: In Vietnam, my elder sister experienced discrimination in education. But when I grew up there was much less discrimination. So I feel fortunate. In South Vietnam we are influenced by the French, and there may be more equality for women than in Central or North Vietnam. In Saigon where I attended the French High School, girls were considered equal to boys. But in Buddhist temples we were told that we needed to be reborn several times to become a man. I always said, "Oh, I don't care to be a man. I would not feel superior if I were a man, and I do not feel inferior as a woman."

SM: Even without overt oppression, I think it's still helpful for women to see you as an example of a woman who is acting out of a lot of strength.

CK: Here in the west in the monastery or nunnery I know that they do not have discrimination against women. And so I behave equally. But when I go to Vietnamese Temples where there are male monks, I try to behave according to the tradition. Not because I'm a hypocrite, but I want to give joy to them.

Alan Senauke: Do nuns take the same precepts as monks?

CK: I'll tell you. I asked Thay (Thich Nhat Hanh) why women have to take 348 precepts instead of 248 precepts like men. Is there discrimination in Buddhism? In *Old Path White Cloud*, Thay explains. A woman went home alone through the forest and was almost raped by a man. So from that day on, the nuns kept one more precept than the monks: You're not allowed to go out alone. The additional precepts are for protecting women, not because women are inferior.

The second thing Thay said was that at the time of the Buddha, women were oppressed by the society. When Buddha accepted women in the order that was a big revolution. But even so, for two thousand years people have continued to believe that woman is inferior to man. And so they think that more precepts for women mean that women are inferior. But we have to see that the extra precepts are for protecting women first.

There is another point that no other teacher has explained but Thay. When the stepmother of the Buddha asked to be ordained as a nun, Buddha at first refused her. She was a queen, and she had even more power over the country than the king. Buddha knew that she was strong and skillful. He said, "I'm worried that if my mother joins the community, she may rule everything."

Then Ananda begged him to ordain her, and the whole community begged him, and Buddha ordained her with the condition that she agree to practice the Eight Observations of Respect that nuns have to observe towards Buddhist monks. That was for controlling her, not because she was inferior, but because she was so strong.

AS: So then these rules became institutionalized.

CK: Yes, but in Plum Village, we do not observe them because Thay says that these Eight Observations were invented to help the stepmother of the Buddha only. He says you need to keep the 14 precepts properly. That's all. But of course he doesn't despise the traditional precepts. And I can accept them just to give joy to the monks who practice in the traditional way. If I can give them joy, I will have a chance to share my insights about women with them, and then they will be unblocked in their understanding.

AS: It's very delicate.

SM: It makes me think of a story you tell in your book about when you first met Thay. You were working in the slums of Saigon at the time, and you were wearing an old dress that didn't fit you very well. Thay said that you should wear a dress that was simple but lovely. You were surprised because you were trying to dress in a way that would make the people in the slums feel comfortable with you. Could you say any more about that?

CK: Thay was not against me going to the slums with a poor dress on. But I wore the same dress everywhere, and I was very proud of working with poor people. Every Sunday I went to hear Thay's dharma talk in a huge temple. About 500 students came, and all of them were dressed beautifully. It was not a slum. But I dressed in my old gray, baggy dress. When Thay called me in, I cried, because I was so proud that I worked with the poor.

AS: So wearing poor clothes was a mark of arrogance?

CK: Yes, it was like saying, "I'm not like other people. I work with the poor." But Thay said, "You should behave in a normal way. You don't have to wear a fancy dress, but when you are among students you, too, should look decent and simple." But in the slum I could wear the dress of the slum people.

SM: And now you wear your nun's robe and shave your head, and it's appropriate for whatever situation you're in, isn't it?

CK: Yes. Unconsciously, I missed Vietnam and the image of a poor nun in a brown dress walking in remote areas to help children. So, I shaved my head and put on my nun's robe as a kind of going home. Some of my friends in the West say, "I miss your hair." When some Vietnamese monks came to the

United States they decided to have long hair and wear American clothes, so as not to shock the eyes of people. At first I did that too, but slowly I changed my mind, because when a monk wears non-monk clothing, it's fake. And when it's fake, it will not inspire confidence. At first our shaved heads may shock people, but if we walk mindfully, beautifully, what is inside will radiate and people will stop and ask, "Who are you?" And humbly we can explain.

SM: You move with a lot of dignity and grace.

CK: We have to, because when you wear the monk's robe you have to behave in the best way you can. If you move in an agitated way, you do more harm than help.

AS: I find that dressing as a priest, shaving my head, raises a very good question. Who is that person? And when you ask, "Who is that person?" you also ask, "Who am I?" So the monk becomes a mirror.

CK: Buddhism teaches that most of our perceptions are erroneous. We may think we understand something thoroughly, but we have to look more deeply. For example, you see a snake and you run away, filled with fear. But when you are angry at your partner, don't think that he is a snake. Look more deeply. Maybe he is only a rope. Too often, with our beloved ones, our son or husband, our daughter or wife, we only see the snake, not the rope.

In meditation we look deeply alone. But sometimes we cannot look deeply enough by ourselves and we have to ask the other person, "If I have hurt you, please try to breathe deeply and calm yourself first, and then come and tell me, and I will try my best to understand and correct my behavior, so that I will not take you for a snake, but a real rope."

AS: Keeping in mind the snake, which is actually a rope, I'd like to ask you a question about the present human rights situation in Vietnam. Because it seems so confrontational. In terms of the communist government there, is there a part of it that's just a rope, not a snake?

CK: Our friends are in jail in Vietnam. And we try to understand that it is because the government takes us for a snake instead of a rope. Our friends in Vietnam have not been able to make it clear enough to the officials that they are not working for political power but for human rights.

AS: They didn't declare it in a skillful enough way?

CK: Maybe. However, if one side, especially the powerful side, is too sure of their wrong perception, it is difficult for the rope to reveal itself!

AS: Do you worry about what Western development will do to Vietnam when the embargo is lifted, which will probably be soon?

CK: The developers are already there.

AS: The country is wide open.

CK: There are many problems. Sometimes I feel overwhelmed. But I try to work one day at a time. If we just worry about the big picture, we are powerless. So my secret is to start right away doing whatever little work I can do. I try to give joy to one person in the morning, and remove the suffering of one person in the afternoon. That's enough. When you see you can do that, you continue, and you give two little joys, and you remove two little sufferings, then three, and then four. If you and your friends do not despise the small work, a million people will remove a lot of suffering. That is the secret. Start right now.

SM: I have one more question. What is it that gives you the most satisfaction in the work that you do?

CK: Twelve years ago, Thay asked me that same question, and I told him, "I enjoy communicating with the children in Vietnam. I enjoy wrapping the parcels of food and feeling close to them." And Thay said, "You cannot cling to this. You have to be prepared to die tomorrow without regret." And I said, "I am the only one who knows all these addresses, and if I die, who will take care of them?" He said, "Life is preparing the way for others to replace you." And I decided to write the book *Learning True Love* for that reason, so I can share what I have learned. Now I can have joy.

But I don't always feel happy. Even in our sangha in Plum Village we are not always at peace. When one sister or brother is unstable, the whole community is affected. So we try to be always fresh and happy and when somebody is sad, you have the serenity to overcome the difficulty.

When the fire inspectors came to Plum Village last February and wanted to close it, I tried to be calm and go slowly. They said we needed to spend about two million dollars to bring Plum Village up to code, or we would have to close. Thay reminded us, if we have to close, we can close. We don't need to run after two million dollars. And now it turns out that we don't have to raise that much money after all. About $500,000 is still needed. And we are just doing what we have to, slowly.

I can enjoy everything now. For me, walking is a joy, sitting is a joy. Having something to eat at mealtime is a joy. Touching the light switch and seeing the dark room bright with light is a joy. And I remember that we have a good sangha and a good teacher. My health is also good. There is so much joy for me.

THE REAL THING — PUNE, INDIA — MARCH 2010

IT'S THE REAL THING

1.

Manerplaw used to lie along the Moie River in Burma, not a half mile from the Thai side of the river, but its geographic isolation seemed nearly complete to me. I journeyed there in the Spring of 1992, with a witness delegation of monks and laypeople from the International Network of Engaged Buddhists, INEB's third delegation to the Burmese border. It was an hour or two boat ride down the Salween and Moie from Mae Son Lap, a dirt road border crossing for timber, cattle, and necessities on the Thai side. From Mae Son Lap south there was dense forest on both shores, with a few deserted lumber mills and several Karen military checkpoints where very young boys stood about with dangling cheroots and haphazardly pointed Kalashnikov rifles. They would never know real childhood.

Manerplaw then, in 1992, was headquarters for the Karen National Union (which had been at war for more than forty years), for our friends from the All Burma Young Monks Union, for the factionalized All Burma Student Democratic Front, and for the National Coalition Government for the Union of Burma, the NCGUB, which functioned as the umbrella for a government in exile. There was an uneasy but necessary cooperation among these and other groups headquartered along two miles of riverbank. Cooperation was necessary because Burmese troops from the State Law and Order Restoration Council (SLORC) had vowed to capture Manerplaw before the rainy season arrived. On Sleeping Dog Mountain, a ridge several miles west, fierce battles were raging. From Manerplaw we could hear the thump of mortar fire and artillery. It was all so vivid and unfamiliar to me that I couldn't even muster an appropriate sense of danger.

We spent three days in Manerplaw, talking with leaders from various groups, meeting soldiers from the front in makeshift tea shops, looking at energy and agricultural projects, thinking about how we could share what we were seeing and learning with our friends at home. On the second night we were invited to dinner at NCGUB headquarters, which consisted of a few hastily framed buildings in a small clearing. We met with Dr. Sein Win, Aung San Suu Kyi's cousin and prime minister of the NCGUB, and a few other officials from the Karen and NCGUB. I don't remember the briefing or conversation, I don't remember the dinner itself. I have had quite a few generous and tasty meals in such settings, eating with a painful awareness that such food was precious and not available to most people.

What I do remember with startling clarity is that bottles of Pepsi Cola were handed around with some ceremony. I felt bound to accept, yet deeply confused. These bottles must have been carried down river with difficulty; the empties would be carted back. Our research into U.S. investment had hardly begun then, but the Americans there knew that Pepsi was the most visible U.S. corporation doing business inside Burma itself, a clear target for our organizing efforts at home. How were we to accept this offering?

And how to understand the pervasive quality of Western tases and goods that seemed to blind even our revolutionary hosts to what they were serving us? Maybe they simply wished to make us feel at home. Maybe they needed the sugar and caffeine. I failed to ask, so my questions are unanswered.

Manerplaw is gone now. It was not captured that winter, though the day we left Burmese military planes attacked by air for the first time. Two years later it fell, with a devastating, disordering effect on Burma's forces of democracy. Pepsi sold its interest in the Rangoon bottling plant, and many other U.S.

businesses have closed up shop there. When business and human rights become tangled up, the bottom line is vulnerable. That is what corporations pay attention to.

2.

Surin is in the Issan region, Thailand's impoverished northeast, half a day by train or bus from Bangkok. It is the devastated and deforested heartland of hardscrabble farming. Most of the trees are gone now and many of the people. There is little to eat in the long dry season, and able-bodied people head for Bangkok and other cities, hoping to find work in sweatshops or in the sex trade.

Luang Por Nan is a Theravada monk, abbot of Wat Sammaki and several other temples in the area that provide a resource and refuge for local people whose lives are prey to poverty, alcoholism, and violence. He is a social experimenter, which is uncommon among monks of any culture. How well these experiments are working out is unclear to me, but it was encouraging to see a local rice bank and small processing plant which packages organic brown rice for sale in Europe, a fertilizer bank where people can share commonly needed resources, and several cooperative stores for basic goods at the village level.

The INEB conference met at Luang Por Nan's temple in 1994, just as the hot season arrived. We had an exposure trip to several of the local coops. One coop had been destroyed by a fire, which took out the store's whole inventory — a costly loss for poor farmers. With great difficulty they rebuilt the inventory and established a new site for the business. Our gaggle of monks, nuns, and foreigners were honored guests at the opening ceremony, a *sadaokro* designed to purge suffering and restore energetic happiness. The monks chanted and received offerings. There was song and dance. A large pavilion where the ceremony was set was crisscrossed with white strings signifying good health and fortune. Villagers delighted in tying these around our wrists, conveying their own joy and welcome with warm smiles and playful insistence. I left with nine cords on my arm. It took many months for the last of them to fall away.

After the ceremony we visited the store itself, and bought a few small treats. A bus returned us to the temple. There I saw the banner strung across the narrow paved road. "Coca Cola welcomes The International Network of Engaged Buddhists." What would Sulak Sivaraksa — INEB's Siamese founder and fierce Buddhist social critic — make of this? It seemed like a bad joke, and yet so believable in a world where image counts as substance, the real thing. Why should this be surprising anymore?

3.

When Vietnam was finally opened to American investment a few years back, U.S. newspapers heralded "Cola Wars between Coke and Pepsi in the streets of Saigon." Coke and Pepsi had bottling plants poised for production the moment trade was sanctioned. They gave out free samples on street corners. Twenty years after the decisive trouncing of American forces and their disorderly flight from Vietnam, the war for hearts and minds was renewed. The corporations have a good shot at winning this war, not with vengeance, but with a carefully considered assault on the soft drink market, one place where the money is and where Western corporate culture can find a firm foothold. This is what America really went to war about thirty years ago: the opening of international markets, the conversion of regional tastes and production to a thirst for one commodified global taste. This is a war that America will most likely win. And we all will lose. What is the real thing?

4. My friends Melody and Latifa journeyed to Pakistan and Afghanistan early in 2002, researching biographical information and collecting stories about Meena, the young woman who founded the Revolutionary Association of Women of Afghanistan in 1977. Meena was assassinated by KGB agents in 1987. Melody relates that in Afghanistan there were no working phones in homes, no aspirin or acetaminophen for aches and pains. But when she met with Meena's comrades in their homes for dinner, there was Coke on the table. Back in Pakistan — where the dangers were even higher for radical women, advocates for democracy and human rights — RAWA women served Pepsi.

5. The real thing is not Coke, the one taste is not Pepsi. These soft drinks began many years ago as patent remedies. Today we are seeing the hucksterism of a medicine show that has gone far beyond our imagination into unconscious realms of desire and delusion. Drink this and you will be forever young and beautiful. Revolutionaries in Burma and Afghanistan, activist monks in Thailand, and even Americans can hardly see how meaning has been stolen from us and replaced by corporate logos and empty illusions. This is not just semiotics, either. Coke and Pepsi addict us to sugar and caffeine, and rot our teeth. Slow poison on several levels.

What is the antidote? How can we gain control of culture and consciousness? What is the real thing? I leave these as open questions. We will be addressing them for many years to come.

THE WORLD FAITHS DEVELOPMENT DIALOGUE — REFLECTIONS ONE YEAR LATER

Oh, the hours we spent inside the Coliseum,
Dodging lions and wasting time....
— from "When I Paint My Masterpiece" by Bob Dylan

A year has come and gone since I traveled to Rome to take part in a meeting sponsored by the World Bank — the World Faiths Development Dialogue (WFDD). If nothing else, I enjoyed the trip, meeting with spiritual activists from numerous faiths, engaging in earnest talk, eating wonderful food, simply being in Rome (which, from my own skewed perspective, I saw as a city of happy New Yorkers) and walking the ancient streets. Was I partaking of the international banking system's largesse? I guess so.

The aim of this Rome meeting and subsequent gatherings (which I followed, but did not attend) has been to shape a definition of poverty and development that includes spiritual values; to offer a faith-based vision to the *World Development Report 2000* (WDR); and help redefine the World Bank's work.

In Rome we spent two days discussing the nature of poverty, in fact, the varieties of poverty. My own perspective, the first noble truth of poverty, follows a definition offered at the meeting by Bishop Diarmuid Martin of the Pontifical Council for Justice & Peace: "Poverty is the inability of people to realize their potential."

Less commonly held, and not at all spoken in Rome or at any of the other WFDD gatherings, is a second noble truth of poverty. The cause of poverty is a systematic clinging to material wealth, manifesting primarily (though not exclusively) as a global corporate capitalist system. The World Bank, along with the International Monetary Fund, the World Trade Organization, and various transnational private and pseudo-public institutions are integral to that cause.

So, on to the third and fourth noble truths of poverty — and here is where my thinking, before and after this meeting, needs to go further: Is there really a path of liberation from poverty, and what are the stages of that path? How do we prioritize resources so they go first to the desperately poor, like those people I have seen in Bangladesh or on the Thai-Burma border? In relation to the World Bank, can we actually transform the Bank's actual legacy of poverty *creation*, or is the presence of religious representatives simply window dressing, helping the Bank to look good and feel good about itself? This has been my concern. The progressive intentions and influence of James Wolfensohn, present Bank president, the assumption of many of the Bank's customary responsibilities by private industry, and the ongoing attempt to wrestle with realities of abject poverty have pointed to a possibility of change. On the other hand, economic modeling and a deeply entrenched career management level at the Bank make change difficult. And more deeply, as my friend Paul Francis, who works for the Bank, has commented, "We have to remember that the Bank is still a bank." That is, even though it has much greater policy flexibility than conventional banks, its loans must still be repaid with interest. If it fails in that mission, then the World Bank will soon find itself without sources of funds to lend out.

At the December 1998 meeting I offered four suggestions for the WFDD's work:

1. Urge the World Bank to support and involve itself in the creation of non-standard indicators that are co-created by poor people themselves, in hope that such new indicators might speak to the Bank's economists and policy makers in human terms that are compelling and intelligible in their own intellectual context.

2. Similarly, the Bank could commit itself to processes for fully including the people most affected in the evaluation of all projects in developing countries. True inclusion is empowerment, going beyond the circles of self-serving government officials and technocrats. This leads to real accountability — to lenders, borrowers, and to the poor themselves. This is risky in two dimensions. First, there is always the risk that empowerment will create new privileged groups. Second, real empowerment might threaten the institution itself, removing power from the hands of those individuals and nations that hold it now.

3. Put debt reduction high on our agenda. In the heavily indebted nations, home to a large portion of the world's six billion, poor people are triple-burdned by an enormous debt service, lack of social services, and absence of benefits that might have come from failed Bank projects. This is a focal point that others in WFDD do not agree with as our agenda. They point out there are many other organizations advocating debt relief. WFDD's mission should be to raise wider concerns about Bank policy and methods. But I can't see how the issue of debt can be set apart from any central questioning about poverty.

4. And this was my main suggestion. As people of faith and trust, WFDD could organize an ongoing process of retreats or councils, real dialogue, where all parties to the World Bank's work — borrowers, lenders, local people, economists, engineers, and people of faith can meet each other as individuals,

with all the joys, sorrows, gifts, needs, and suffering that mark our human lives, and come to a better understanding of the systems we function within. This, I think, is a Buddhist approach — deep listening as essential to a social action path, part of the fourth noble truth of poverty.

Well, those were my naive suggestions, rooted in my own perhaps willful misunderstanding of the word "dialogue" in "World Faiths Development Dialogue." I felt that simple revisions in the *World Development Report*, no matter how well-intentioned, would have no real impact on the Bank's action. In the end, these revisions were ultimately rejected by the Bank, and the key WDR editors resigned. That was WFDD's main agenda, which I didn't quite understand at the time.

It was disappointing, too, that beyond the meeting in Rome, which truly was collegial and interesting, I have found little dialogue within the group. The postings and comments I sent out by e-mail to all were only answered by the compassionate, dedicated, and overworked WFDD coordinator Wendy Tyndale. There was not the kind of give and take, rubbing and polishing that I see as necessary for a lively intellectual process. Meeting notes, articles, comments seem to have been funneled to the few people assigned to drafting our response to the WDR. Further meetings —like the Washington, DC gathering of church leaders with the Bank president and the Archbishop of Canterbury in November 1999 — come off without any notification to some us who had earlier been involved in the process. In that sense, our own workings have mirrored the Bank's wondrous ability to create hierarchies of privilege and to crunch numbers and ideas.

So, can we really make a change in the vision and function of the World Bank? I would have to say: no, not this way. And can the Bank fulfill its high-minded mission —"A World Free of Poverty"— and still be a bank? Again, no. Something new is needed. New thinking, entirely outside the box of development. With years of Buddhist practice behind me, it is challenging to face the anger that comes up for me each time I just hear the word "development," a word that usually means the very opposite of what it connotes.

Last month I was speaking with a friend who directs a watchdog organization that tracks nuclear weapons design, proliferation, and production work at Los Alamos Nuclear Laboratory. He described various dialogues initiated by the lab in recent years. Dialogues on the environment, on economic issues, on security, all consciously or unconsciously serving to deflect attention and grassroots organizing from the central issues of nuclear weapons and political power. Some of these efforts were led by good, sincere people at the lab, not simply calculating manipulators. The Los Alamos powers that be, though, went even further, luring board members of my friend's organization with well-paid positions and interesting projects. As he related this, I couldn't help thinking about parallels to the WFDD process.

But interesting and encouraging things are happening nonetheless. Last June a massive lobbying effort convinced the World Bank to delay funding and implementation of controversial plans (part of the China Western Poverty Reduction Project) to resettle Chinese and Muslim farmers on the Tibetan Plateau.

Novelist Arundhati Roy's essay, "For The Greater Common Good" is alerting the world to the depredations of the Bank-financed Narmada River Dam in India. In the middle of November, against long political odds, a coalition of Episcopal, Catholic, and Protestant churches successfully pushed the U.S. Congress to support a package of IMF debt relief for poor countries, an effort that will likely leverage much more extensive debt relief from the G7 lenders to IMF.

The dust has not settled at the 1999 round of World Trade Organization talks in Seattle. This globalization summit was met by activists with an intense and well-planned protest effort that veered into violence. While I felt dismayed at the police violence in Seattle, and at the anger and vandalism of what the media chooses to call "anarchist thugs," the structural violence of the WTO, the World Bank, IMF, etc. is incalculably more destructive of life and freedom than the streetfighting. In a way, I find the protests, particularly the large and under-reported nonviolent protest in Seattle, deeply encouraging. That this degree of awareness and motivation focuses on a pivotal mechanism of global capitalism means people are coming to a broader and clearer awareness of how things really work.

So there is good news afoot, and it is based on grassroots organizing, not on noble-sounding rhetoric. If we truly want to reduce poverty we need to be allies to the poor, give space to their voices and demands. Let's invite them to our cathedrals, temples, and high-rise meeting rooms. Then the fun begins.

— November 1999

THE WORLD IS WHAT YOU MAKE IT: ONE ZENNIST'S VIEW OF GLOBAL RESPONSIBILITY

We offer ourselves to ourselves, and we offer others to others. The causal relation of giving (dana) has a power that pervades the heavens above and the human world below... Entrusting flowers to the wind, and entrusting birds to the season may also be the meritorious action of giving.

— Zen Master Eihei Dogen
From "Bodaisatta Shishobo"
"The Bodhisattva's Four
Embracing Dharmas" (1243 C.E.)

Looking around this troubled planet, we see fierce and unusual weather — last year's Cylone Nargis in Burma, 2005's Hurricane Katrina in the U.S., unprecedented storms flooding low-lying areas of Asia, and tornados sweeping across the American Midwest. The slow but measurable warming of oceans is breaking up age-old glaciers in Greenland, Iceland, Canada, and the arctic regions. Inland, drought is steadily sucking away lakes and wetlands, leaving whole populations to fight over diminishing water resources. Where I live, in California, we now have a year-round season of wildfires. The future bodes more of the same.

Sixty-five years ago, human technology "developed" to the point where nuclear weapons gave us the means to destroy earthly civilization in one blow. After an initial murderous experiment with atomic bombs in Hiroshima and Nagasaki, we have — so far — taken the road of nuclear deterrence, refraining from further use of such weapons. But our heedless pattern of consumption, our seemingly unquenchable appetite for fossil fuels, leads us to destroy an environment that has sheltered us for age after age. In geological time, the present environmental destruction flowing from human activity over less than a hundred years — the massive generation of CO_2 and resultant global warming — is as swift as a nuclear bomb, and potentially as destructive to life.

From our narrow human perspective on time, global warming seems to have come on slowly. But this is hardly the case. A public awareness that we, people, are causing global warming is something new, hardly discussed even by scientists until the 1970s. Today, though, it seems to be settled science. But despite high-minded government rhetoric and self-congratulatory hoopla about the supposed "greening" of multinational corporations, our addiction to fossil fuels has hardly waned. In fact, the Third World is increasingly folded into a technological and consumerist global economy, swelling the world's appetite for oil, coal, natural gas, and deforested agricultural land.

Let's change gears here...When the Buddha awakened, so long ago, his original teachings turned on the wheel of *paticca samuppada* or, in English, dependent origination. The ins and outs of dependent origination are highly complex but its core principle has been clearly expressed in early Buddhist texts.

When this is, that is.
From the arising of this comes the arising of that.
When this isn't, that isn't.
From the cessation of this comes the cessation of that.

The Buddha's early teachings pointed to dependent origination as the driving wheel of birth, death, and rebirth. In traditional Buddhist terms, this is seen as playing out in each individual life after life. Towards the middle of this wheel we find six realms of existence into which beings are born. The realm of Hungry Ghosts or *pretas* features ghastly beings with huge, swollen bellies and long, pencil-thin necks. They are insatiably hungry, but unable to swallow the food they crave. *Pretas* are driven by illusory appetites and desires that can never be fulfilled or satisfied. We all know people like this, who are never satisfied, never have enough material riches and things.

From the vantage point of engaged Buddhism, with its structural and systemic view of dependent origination, present-day corporate globalization is exactly an expression of how the Buddha's wheel of dependent origination gives rise to whole nations, peoples, and cultures born and reborn in the realm of hungry ghosts. I live in such a nation. It is called the United States.

I single out the United States because it is my country, our country, and hopefully that is where my engaged Buddhist practice and political work are most likely to have an impact. The U.S. uses between 25 to 30% of the world's annual energy resources to support roughly 5% of the world's population. Our 200,000,000 cars and trucks, most of which are older and less than fuel efficient, account for almost half of the world's CO_2 emissions. In 2004, U.S. vehicles generated the equivalent of 314,000,000 metric tons of carbon. Imagine a coal train 55,000 miles long, stretching around the globe twice! Half of our electricity comes from aging coal-fired power plants, which, along with vast amounts of CO_2, release large quantities of sulfur dioxide and mercury, causing acid rain and toxicity. So-called "clean coal technologies" are still far in the future. In the agricultural sector, chemical fertilizers and waste products from ruminant animals account for 10% of U.S. greenhouse gases, far surpassing the impact of agriculture in other parts of the world. As the saying goes, we live "high on the hog." And people around the world pay the price for our lifestyle.

Consider Cyclone Nargis, which devastated Burma in May of 2008. A U.S.-based meteorologist called Nargis, "...one of those once-in-every-500-years kind of things." But the Centre for Science and Environment (CSE), a respected Indian environmental monitoring group, sees Cyclone Nargis as a direct effect of global warming, a sign of things to come. Sunita Narain of CSE said "The victims of these cyclones are climate change victims, and their plight should remind the rich world that it is doing too little to contain its greenhouse gas emissions." He added that large-scale polluters bear responsibility for what is happening in Burma. If this is true, then our connection to Burma, and other nations where unforeseen storms, floods, and drought are appearing with greater frequency, is a matter of dependent origination — "because there is this, that arises" — cause and effect. Could it be that the cyclone's devastation arises from our addiction to fossil fuels, which causes global warming, rising sea levels, and new weather patterns? Global warming is just one effect of our addiction to fossil fuels. Our hunger for Burma's oil and natural gas (along with the energy appetite of developing nations like China, India, and Thailand) is precisely what provides Burma's brutal military dictatorship the economic leverage to stay in power. I do not wish to live by stealing the natural resources of impoverished people half a world away or by causing the environmental destruction that endangers everyone, myself included. If our national habits of consumption contribute to world's hardships, then what are we to do?

The Zen Buddhist tradition, as passed down to us in the West from China and Japan, is, like Tibetan Buddhism, an expression of bodhisattva practice. Bodhisattvas vow to save beings from suffering, reaching out, warm hand to warm hand. We live this vow by following the bodhisattva's moral precepts of thought, speech, and action — no killing, stealing, lying, intoxicating, and so on. These are precepts of relationship, of giving and receiving. As Zen Master Dogen says: "We offer ourselves to ourselves, and we offer others to others." These principles can guide our actions as individuals, communities, and nations.

Here are some practices for healing the world. These are not solutions, but tools for looking at ourselves and what we do. Each of them is nearly impossible to realize. I take this phrase — "nearly impossible" — as a challenge to do all that I can.

* * *

• The bodhisattva precepts boil down to one essential principle: not to live at the expense of other beings. This is simple to say, and very difficult to do.

• Each of us must take complete responsibility for the world, as if the world's fate depended on our words and actions. Whether we know it or not, it does.

• An old Zen teaching says, "Not knowing is most intimate." But this is different from knowing nothing or willfully closing one's eyes. Considering the suffering of myself and others, naturally I study everything I can find. As I study and perhaps feel I am developing some mastery or understanding, right there I should know that my understanding is incomplete and will always be so. That incompleteness is "not knowing." To accept that about oneself and to press on is to be intimate with the world.

• Act mindfully and correctly, irrespective of results. Do things because they are the proper things to do. It may seem as if one's own modest efforts at conservation have no impact, but recall the Jataka tale in which a parrot carried water, drop by drop, to save his forest from spreading fires. His single-minded and seemingly hopeless dedication inspired a god's tears, which quenched the flames.

• Thinking globally, acting locally is good, but limited. One must also think locally and act globally. That means simultaneously working to curb consumption at home, at work, in one's town, and pushing our elected representatives to enact legislation and policies that have impact on a national and international level. Our national moral authority flows from a willingness to make personal sacrifices.

• "Entrusting flowers to the wind, and entrusting birds to the season..." When I recognize that my life and everything in it has been freely given to me, how can I deny this gift to all other beings, and to the planet itself? Take only what one needs and allow all things to be free and fully themselves.

* * *

I have no idea if such practices and policies will prove successful. Despite the efforts of our best minds and most powerful computers, we don't know what the future will bring.

But the world is what you make it...

ON RACE & BUDDHISM

Zen Master Dogen wrote, "Gourd with its tendrils is entwined with gourd." This means we are all intimately bound up, wound up with each other. Truly inseparable. At Buddhist Peace Fellowship, San Francisco Zen Center, and at Berkeley Zen Center, we have been talking about the complexities of diversity, race, Zen practice, and our communities in the United States. This is not just about "political correctness." It is about practice and awareness. My own thoughts are not entirely clear. If I sound critical, it includes self-criticism. My own efforts have fallen short and I think we need to work on this together.

After six years of practice, homeless among householders, way-seekers, and mendicant teachers, the Buddha sat under the Bodhi Tree with the firm intention of awakening. After seven days he perceived the true nature of birth and death, the chain of causation, and awakened to realization with the morning star. At that moment he spoke these words: "Wondrous! I now see that all beings everywhere have the wisdom and virtues of the enlightened ones, but because of misunderstandings and attachments they do not realize it."

Allowing his understanding to ripen, allowing *bodhicitta*, the mind of compassion to ripen, he took up the responsibilities of teaching, sharing his experience in a way that unlocked the mystery of our own experience. As the Buddha came to express it, "I simply teach about the nature of suffering and the end of suffering." This is a radical teaching. It goes to the root. His understanding that all beings everywhere have the wisdom and virtues of the enlightened ones leaves us today with a great responsibility. As the wheel of Mahayana Dharma turned, that responsibility was further clarified by the Bodhisattva vow to save all beings. And yet this vow was there from the beginning. Why else did the Buddha rise from the comfort and joy of enlightenment and freedom to teach? Why else did he offer teachings like the "Metta Sutta" where he says:

> May all beings be happy.
> May they be joyous and live in safety.
> All living beings, whether weak or strong,
> in high or middle or low realms of existence,
> small or great, visible or invisible,
> near or far, born or to be born,
> let no one deceive another, nor despise any being in any state;
> let none by anger or hatred wish harm to another.
> Even as a mother at the risk of her life watches over
> and protects her only child,
> so with a boundless mind should one cherish all living things,
> suffusing love over the entire world, above, below,
> and all around, without limit;
> so let one cultivate an infinite good will toward the whole world.

True to that teaching, he offered refuge to everyone he met on the path. Kings and paupers, ascetics and householders, people of all castes, brahmins, outcasts, and criminals. After some strenuous convincing, he offered refuge to women. That's a long story in itself, not unrelated to the issue at hand today. The Buddha's reluctance reminds us that patriarchy has deep roots running through most cultures.

Taking refuge means committing your life to waking up, to taking on the problem of suffering and ending suffering for all beings and ourselves. This is what zazen is about. Sitting upright in stillness means to see oneself in complete interdependence with all beings, with the rocks and trees and ocean and sky. The emptiness we so often talk about is not some kind of negative space. It is total interdependence. "Gourd with its tendrils entwined with gourd." True reality is empty of any one thing, empty of self, because all things, all people co-create each other.

Seeing through and beyond dualistic thinking is the direct *experience* of zazen. I underscore the word 'experience,' because, if we are caught by our ideas or an idle wish, we slip back into the tide of duality. All of us have such experiences from time to time. A moment of merging with someone or something we love, a moment of doing something completely, a moment of losing oneself in meditation. At times in zazen we settle fully into the realm of nonduality and recognize that this is our true mind, our true state of being. All the great spiritual traditions express an understanding of this natural way of life.

By habit we see the world dualistically. Driven by doubt and fear, by a lack of trust in our true Mind, we see things as self and objects, as <u>us and them</u>, as other. It seems so hard to recognize the truth that Tibetan Buddhists teach: that every being was at one time my own mother. The root of racism is denial of this truth. It is about seeing people as *other* in a systemic way. Seeing people as objects is such an entrenched habit we are not usually aware of it. I would emphasize the word "systemic," because ideas are like a virus in society. They have a power that goes beyond our individual like and dislike. Racism is a system of domination that is economic and political as well as personal. It runs deep in the oppressor and the oppressed alike, but the damage caused is different.

Even though I have the privilege of a good education, middle class male upbringing, and white skin, I find in myself deeply ingrained survival responses as someone born a Jew. Several years ago at a meeting of international Buddhist activists in Thailand I realized that by evening of the first day I had figured out who among the Westerners was Jewish. And I realized that all the Jews were doing the same thing and had "signified" to each other. We knew who each other was, and we were more comfortable for it. This, I am sure, is a pattern that goes back through centuries of ghetto life, of being seen as the other by a dominant culture. It's not a genetic thing. I can still remember sitting in the den at home, my mother telling me how to watch out for myself at school. She explained that some people would exclude and threaten me just for being Jewish. It's so deep that sometimes I often find myself looking around the zendo and counting those I think are Jewish. Some of you may find yourself making a similar census. I know that people of color do this.

But let's remember where our Buddhism came from. Our ancestors come from India, China, and Japan. When I visit Suzuki Roshi's temple in Japan, Rinso-in, I always walk in the graveyard where the old priests of the temple were buried. How amazing it is for Zen to leap oceans and cultures and be so generously offered to us. We should accept it humbly, recognizing the price of suffering paid to plant the Dharma seed here. We owe it to our teachers and ourselves to share this practice with the same generosity and open-mindedness. Keep in mind that most Buddhists even in America don't look like me. They are Chinese, Japanese, Thai, Vietnamese, and so on. I come to Buddhism out of suffering. They come to Buddhism by birth.

How does it feel to come to Zen practice as a person of color? And such people will come; they do come. My friend Sala Steinbach, an African-American practitioner at San Francisco Zen Center, says, "If it is about liberation, people of color will be interested." They are. The Dalai Lama draws stadiums full of people in Mexico. In South America there are Zen and Tibetan teachers with very strong lay sanghas. I ask my Asian and Latino and African-American friends about how it feels to come here, to San Francisco Zen Center or Spirit Rock. And I ask myself what feelings come up to see these friends walk through the doors. Dogen suggests that one take a step back to turn one's light inward and illuminate oneself. What I see in myself is then reflected back into the world.

The answer to how it feels to anyone largely depends on two further interrelated questions. First, does one feel safe and seen in the community? Are the conditions of one's life acknowledged, welcomed, explored in the sangha? I suspect the answer is sometimes yes, and too often no. Thoughtless words can turn people from the temple and from the practice. I have seen this happen. An offhand comment is made about how we are all white and middle class here in the meditation hall, with people of color and working class friends sitting right there. When we unknowingly see through a lens of class and white supremacy, people are made to feel invisible and uncounted.

White supremacy is the cornerstone of racism, created out of blindness to one's (my) own privilege as a white man. It is at once personal and systemic. If one wants to see white supremacy, the practice of turning our light inward needs to be combined with dialogue with friends and sangha members who don't carry this very particular privilege.

The same kinds of painful things happen if you are homosexual, or if by reason of injury or fact of birth you can't get up the steps of the temple. Blindness to oppression hurts and turns people away. That's what it might feel like from one side.

On the other side, the Buddha's understanding is "all beings have the wisdom and virtues of the enlightened ones, but because of misunderstandings and attachments they do not realize it." This understanding is so precious that we are obligated to share it. I don't mean crude proselytizing, but the Buddha himself never stopped preaching dharma. Now we have centers and institutions for dharma. To make zazen and dharma available, we need to tell people they are welcome and invite them to practice with us. We must find ways to open our doors to those who can come to us. Some San Francisco churches have created a kind of covenant of "open congregation." This means that in their literature and at their services, classes, and events they make it known that they welcome people of color, gays and lesbians, and so on. This is being proactive rather than passive on questions of diversity and inclusion.

Already we are taking practice to jails and hospitals, to people who might not be able to come to the meditation hall. We can also take ourselves to mosques, churches, and synagogues, where we can meet with ministers and parishioners. If we make ourselves known there, we will be welcome, and people will appreciate that we have reached across various lines to witness their own practice. More than that, we can learn from other peoples and other traditions, and become more truly human.

This is necessary, because in America passivity means white supremacy. It is subtle and pervasive, conditioned by and conditioning our magazines, movies, television, our clothing, all the things we buy. It is a virus infecting my own mind as a person with so-called privileges, and the mind of someone who might not have such privileges. Recently I was invited to talk about Buddhism and race to a diverse group of teenagers doing an interfaith social action internship in San Francisco. I hope I did a good job talking to them, but it was curious to me that I was the organizers' first choice for a Buddhist speaker. The irony is that Buddhism in America often gets defined as and by people who look like me, not by the far more numerous Asian and Asian-American practitioners.

But the wonderful thing about what the Buddha taught, what we can experience in zazen, is that each of us can go beyond duality. It can't be done just by reason and talk. We have to uncover the reality of the world, which lives deep in our bones, and then bring it back out into the world. We must be willing to make a lot of mistakes. Make our mistakes, learn the lessons and go back at it. The African American scholar/practitioner bell hooks writes about this in *Buddhist Women on the Edge*:

> In a culture of domination, preoccupation with victimhood and identity is inevitable. I once believed that progressive people could analyze the dualities and dissolve them through a process of dialectical critical exchange. Yet

globally the resurgence of notions of ethnic purity, white supremacy, have led marginalized groups to cling to dualisms as a means of resistance....The willingness to surrender to attachment to duality is present in such thinking. It merely inverts the dualistic thinking that supports and maintains domination.

Dualities serve their own interests. What's alarming to me is to see so many Americans returning to those simplistic choices. People of all persuasions are feeling that if they don't have dualism, they don't have anything to hold on to.

If we are concerned with dissolving these apparent dualities we have to identify anchors to hold on to in the midst of fragmentation, in the midst of a loss of grounding. My anchor is love....

I like to think that love and compassion are anchors of my practice. But they depend on mindfulness. Zazen is rooted in mindfulness, breath after breath, thought after thought. This kind of training carries over into life outside the zendo. I try to uncover my own thought patterns. This is sometimes painful and embarrassing, but it is the essence of saving myself and all sentient beings. It is amazing to see the stories one can make up about other people, and how these stories are conditioned by race, or class, or privilege. Check it out for yourself. When you meet someone you consider different from yourself, do you think you know something about them? Do you think you might know the same kinds of things about another white person or someone more like you? This is a mindfulness practice, watching one's thoughts about race, or any kind of difference. I suggest this is for our own sake, and not for the sake of political correctness. This is a very personal practice.

Then we can go further into our extended communities. Ask your friends of color how they experience the practice and the community. This is entering the realm of not knowing — risky, but completely necessary. In the wider Buddhist community, it might mean making excursions and visits to Asian Buddhist temples. They are friendly places. The same dharma resides there, though it may take some different forms. We don't think twice about going to restaurants featuring Asian cuisine.

When we have closely examined ourselves, and begun to look around and share our thoughts with others, then we have started to create the conditions for change. If our whole society could take such steps, it would be the start of a wonderful, hopeful era. Could there be racial peace for the first time in history? This is no pipe dream. It is the bodhisattva vow, the working of our way-seeking mind.

If each of us, and the sanghas we cherish, could nurture this process of mindfulness, the change could come more quickly. Compassion and peace could blossom in very surprising ways. And our life of zazen would be a golden wind blowing across a meadow of wildflowers.

COLUMBIA UNIVERSITY CAMPUS — APRIL 2008

WHAT DID YOU LEARN IN SCHOOL? — 40 YEARS AFTER THE COLUMBIA STRIKE

These are brief reflections of the CU 68 Strike Gathering, April 24-27, 2008. Apologies. This may be too "in-house" for those who don't share the history.

From the moment I walked back onto the Columbia campus — my first time in 30 years — I felt energized by memory, by the warm embraces of old friends, and by the notion that our work was unfinished. It was amazing to gather and review our history, to consider strengths, weaknesses, and the present day implications of our ancient tangled karma. Few people have such an opportunity. There were more than 150 strike veterans present, and without exception, those who chose to come back for this gathering have each tried to live according to the best of what we learned in 1968, setting aside pettiness and narrow views.

• Forty years is a long time. Leaving Egypt, the Jews wandered in the desert for forty years. Long enough, maybe, to disremember God's message, and yet remember there was a God. (Not that I believe there is one, of course.) My own long-term memory is gapped and elusive. It is hard to know what I remember and what I think I remember. For example, my images of the arrests in Low Library, confirmed by several other narratives, seem like a movie I saw long ago. Then I feel the bump on the right side of my head, artifact of police clubbing — photographically visible on this book's back cover — and I know I didn't make this up. I <u>think</u> I remember going backstage after a Grateful Dead concert in Central Park, talking to Jerry Garcia, and inviting the Dead to come play at Columbia. This did happen, but it was Bob Merlis who actually called their road manager and worked out the necessary logistics. I remember being on the strike committee after the bust (I cannot recall a thing about the meetings aside from arguments and boredom). But I can't remember how I got there. Talking with people at the strike gathering, I learned I was a representative from the Low Commune, though how that came down escapes me.

Actually, it was a relief to find that others' memories suffered the same insufficiencies and doubts. God knows what our 50th anniversary might be like.

• I expected to recognize most everyone. The workings of time, gravity, hair loss, and the effects of a high-fat American diet meant that I had to look through an aging face in front of me to see the youthful face within. I said to one old friend, "Yes, but who are you?" Only then could I collate name and face, memory and identity clicking into focus.

But the pure pleasure of old friendship is beyond explanation. Falling so easily into step with Hilton Obenzinger,

Les Gottesman, Rick Winston and others — time seemed to drop away. The present of 1968 and the present of 2008 were contiguous. I felt this way about many others, and savored the mystery of finding myself close to some people I had not known well at all. Maybe growing up (if that's what we have done) has removed barriers to unrealized friendships.

• From the moment Bill Sales, a leader of the Student Afro-American Society (SAS) began to speak about his experience at Columbia and in Hamilton Hall, mists of confusion parted that had long obscured interactions between Black students and SDS. Misunderstanding had lingered for forty years, which is understandable given the bitter facts of white supremacy that go to the root of our American experience. Why exactly had SAS told SDS to leave Hamilton Hall — the first building occupied — and take our own building? But the truth-telling of Ray Brown, Thulani Davis, Al Dempsey, Leon Denmark, Michelle Patrick, and many of the SAS Hamilton Hall veterans brought clarity and tears mixed together.

On Friday night we learned something about what it was like for Black students at Columbia and Barnard back then. We heard about racial profiling at Columbia — students being stopped for i.d. checks over and over again; about stellar athletes who were recruited then not allowed to take the field; about students who had been raised in the segregated South finding segregation alive and well in student housing and even in classes. We were reminded about the ugly *Jester* (the college humor magazine of which I was an associate editor) satire of Columbia's Black fraternity. The most painful thing was to hear SAS members say after forty years that these days at Columbia were the hardest times of their lives. I am sorry to say I never knew that.

Until now I didn't get how Columbia's black students had carried the weight of race on their backs. Their own parents had fought doggedly against oppression in employment, the military, education, and in society at large. These students, come to an elite university, carried all their parents' and communities' best hopes for ending or transcending the sickness of racism. Given the circumstances of their upbringing and all they had learned from their parents' struggles, it is not surprising that SAS brought a strong notion of discipline to the occupation of Hamilton Hall, a style that was very different from the freewheeling participatory democracy of SDS. When SDS left, the first thing the Black occupiers did was to clean Hamilton Hall from top to bottom. *(Although I must say that we — or more accurately the commune women — did a good job keeping Low clean and habitable for a week.)* Ray Brown told Barbara Bernstein:

> ...inherent in discipline, especially in a long-term stay, would be the need to be clean, and to be neat, from everything from food to waste and clothing. And I think there were some deep cultural divisions between at least some of African–American students and the white students. And it's clear we maintained our building in a different way than the other students, and we did that with some pride. But that was a level of discipline that went from making sure that we controlled who was in the building and what was in the building and what was done in the building...everything about your person and your space is critical in a situation that calls for discipline.

For Black students the stakes have always been higher than for white protesters. And they still are. Their hard-won places in the Ivy League were at stake. Even though this was New York City, not the deep South, SAS was well aware of the shooting at a segregation protest near the campus of South Carolina State University in Orangeburg, SC only two months earlier, which left three students dead and twenty-seven wounded. They had a correct perception of themselves as potential victims of state violence. A week before the occupations they saw NYC police reaching for their pistols in a melee at Columbia's gym site.

Going back to the first panel on Thursday evening, Bill Sales explained a central point that was developed by many other Student Afro-American Society veterans throughout the weekend. African-American students at Columbia and Barnard were involved with the wider Black communities in Harlem and Morningside Heights. They participated in local organizing efforts, worked and volunteered in the community, and had friendships that crossed the usual town-gown line. More than Vietnam, the gym was their central issue. How could a public park belonging to the people of New York, the people of Harlem, be co-opted for the nearly exclusive use of an elite university? Black students had links to Manhattan's African-American political leaders. (Can you imagine actual relationships between SDS and city government?) What was clear is that despite the isolation and discrimination these students felt on campus, they saw themselves directly connected to the people and the city around them. This was not something abstract, like having the correct political perspective, but a matter of flesh and blood, brick and soil.

At one of Saturday's panels, Mark Rudd said, "The miracle is that after forty years, the Black students told the white participants what was on their minds. And we heard them." I hope this is true. I hope we heard them, because our future is still at stake.

Paul Spike wrote a moving piece for the Saturday night reading. He spoke of his activist father's unsolved 1966 murder. Then he pressed on to reflect on what he (and I, and so many well-intentioned white students) failed to see right in front of us. I quote some of Paul's words. They go right to the heart of things.

I want to ask Ray Brown, and Thulani, and Leon, and all of your brothers and sisters, to try to forgive me — and those like me. I want to ask all of the black students at Columbia in 1968 to try to forgive the adolescent self-absorption and intellectual mindlessness, even the privileged racism, which failed to grasp the reality of their suffering, which failed to reach out to them.

I realize this is a lot to ask. It is like asking me to forgive the people responsible for my father's murder. I understand that asking for forgiveness is, in many ways, outrageous.

But I believe that, if you could forgive me, and forgive us, then perhaps one day together our children might begin to fulfill the ideals — freedom, justice, equality — which we all want them to share.

Note: Sherry and Kamau Suttles' film "VALA! The Power of Black Students at Columbia University 1968-2008" is an essential document. Prof. Stefan Bradley, of Southern Illinois University, has published journal articles on African-American struggles at Columbia, and his excellent book Harlem vs. Columbia University: Black Student Power in the Late 1960s was published by University of Illinois Press in 2009.

• It is embarrassing to admit how few Barnard women I knew during my four years at Columbia. At last I did have a Barnard girlfriend, and we were beaten and busted together in Low. But there was an amazing collection of women veterans of '68 who came to the gathering. Only one or two could I consider friends from back in the day.

I could chalk this up to psychology or immaturity. My social development was hardly enhanced by smoking a lot of dope. But I suspect it was also, consciously or not, part of the

Columbia plan — isolate and elevate Columbia men to their intended high place in society. Spare them the powerful distraction of women in the halls and classrooms.

What little I knew of Barnard life has been long forgotten. Did I know that Barnard students were locked in each night? You could get expelled for living in sin off campus? (Oh, yes...I did that...) But this was just the tip of the iceberg. A cohort of women — every bit as smart and talented as their male counterparts across Broadway — were denied access to name-brand professors at Columbia. These professors, while inclined to support and encourage Columbia men as future colleagues, tended to belittle and marginalize the few women bold enough to fight for places in their classes. I'm sorry I didn't remember this.

I like to think that the events of 1968 put cracks in the false front of male supremacy at Columbia. It's a comforting thought. The numerous accomplished women who co-organized our gathering and shared all the various stages seem to confirm this. Their creative and intellectual abilities would not stay bottled up.

But there is no erasing the pain of their experience, how long and hard the struggle has been. It is not enough to witness victory over narrow prejudice and contrived circumstance. We should know there are scars on the surface and wounds deep below. And I wonder what tragic lives are unseen — among women, Blacks, and even among the white students? Such stories are too often lost.

• In 1968, we took Low Library easily, climbing in and out the windows, scampering about on ledges. A hundred or more of us slept on the floor for a week...with only one bathroom. If it were today, I imagine looking at each other and thinking: Only one bathroom, maybe we should reconsider. Along with loaves of bread, whole chickens, apples and grapefruit, our allies on the outside would have to toss up cartons of Viagra and FloMax.

• It is safe to say that many of our political perspectives have changed over the last forty years. Still there are unresolved issues around strategies of violent and nonviolent social change. My own views are clear at this point, or at least clearer. I am unwilling to kill or harm another person in the service of my beliefs. This intention flows from a study of Dr. King, Gandhi, the Buddha, and Catholic activists, which replaces the imperfectly understood Leninism and Guevarism I subscribed to in the late 60s and 70s.

But I still believe that political change is inseparably linked to power. This means there are bound to be opposing points of view. In 1957 Dr. King preached:

> Love is creative, understanding goodwill for all men. It is the refusal to defeat any individual. When you rise to the level of love, of its great beauty and power, you seek only to defeat evil systems. Individuals who happen to be caught up in that system you love, but you seek to defeat the system.

Active nonviolence is a difficult path. It involves a soldier's discipline and an awakened faith in human nature, even when seeing human nature at its worst. We have to make use of power. That will not always be pretty or nice, but my hope is that as much as possible we can rely on power <u>with</u>, rather than power <u>over</u>. Something like the Aikido techniques of aligning and turning with one's opponent.

But we are not yet done with the past. Much of Columbia's SDS leadership was only a year or two later instrumental in Weather Underground. I myself was involved in this organization. At the Townhouse explosion — a would-be bomb factory in Greenwich Village — Ted Gold (whom I knew), along with Diana Oughton and Terry Robbins were killed in the service of a militant political line (which I believe was marked by a sincere but deluded identification with the world's oppressed) run off the rails. At several points in the weekend people felt the need to celebrate Weather politics, honoring those who are dead or still imprisoned, perhaps in affirmation that years spent in those ideological wars were not wasted. I can remember and grieve, but I cannot celebrate. Others, of course, were quick to attack.

I have some regrets, but I can't get caught in recriminations over wasted years. Do I wish I/we had a clear vision of nonviolent direct action? That we had built a broad and radical movement that turned America away from war, racism, and destruction of the world's environment? Of course. But I remember the murder of the foremost proponent of that very vision, Martin Luther King. His killing was prelude to the uprising at Columbia. The assassination of King, Malcolm X, Fred Hampton, and other leaders propelled many of us towards armed struggle. Whether one calls this crazy or not (I don't), there was an ineluctable logic to our course. The false logic of trauma keeps one from thinking straight.

Now forty years have passed. We can weep and we can heal. We can honor those we grew up with — right or wrong, alive or dead — just by seeing them as human, neither on or under a pedestal. We remember brothers and sisters still imprisoned, along with two million others caught up in the world's largest gulag, the United States prison system. We can also honor the lives of all those who did show up last week, lives that are astonishing in meaning and variety. And I hope we can build a strong nonviolent movement that weans us from war, from oil, from exploitation, and from self-destruction. Which means we have to train ourselves in nonviolence, and deconstruct the habits of violence that persist in each of us.

• I wonder what would have happened if we had another week together. On one hand I find myself yearning for more time and more opportunity to be with old friends and to engage with our shared and disparate history. On the other hand, it might not have been pretty. We would probably have gotten past the love fest to our disagreements. Those differences nourish the fertile soil of change.

• Thulani Davis and I organized a memorial service on Sunday morning at Earl Hall to remember those connected to Columbia and the strike who have died in the years since 1968. This included participants on all sides and allies in the wider world. Names were read; people spoke briefly of the departed. Mark Rudd and Jeff Sokolow recited Kaddish. Tom Hurwitz read from the Episcopal Book of Hours. Thulani offered Buddhist verses. All this was more or less in the script we created. Unscripted and marvelous, Plunky Branch showed up with a soprano saxophone and a cd player queued to a gospel-style piano track. I remembered his face — that youthful, playful quality bright and clear — from the late 60s Soul Syndicate. I asked what he had in mind, and he said he could play "Amazing Grace." I said, why don't we start the whole thing that way, and so we did. His playing built, the melody down low, rising, twisting, and filling every hollow of Earl Hall. It was impossible to hold back the tears that came along with the music. Then came words and more tears, and Plunky led us home playing Thomas A. Dorsey's gospel classic "Precious Lord, Take My Hand."

• Sunday's chill and bluster was suitable weather for the closing in Morningside Park, though the weather was too iffy for a planned picnic. A small group of stalwarts were left. There were a few speeches that went on too long, then a cherry tree was planted on the hillside, where its blossoms can drift over Harlem below. Again, for me, the park was a place discovered at last. Aside from playing softball for physical education, and going to demonstrate at the gym site in April of 68, I don't think I had ever set foot in Morningside Park, although for three years I lived on 119th Street, just a block away. Another embarrassing realization of how cut off I was from the actual world around me. The park, built in the 1880s and 90s around designs by Olmsted and Vaux, is quite beautiful, with winding paths, green fields, and tall trees. Community activism since the 1980s has recreated an urban gem, hewing to Olmsted's plans. A pond and waterfall now rest in the abandoned excavation of Columbia's ill-considered gym.

• Everything is incomplete. The intensity of being with old comrades, of reconsidering the things we did so long ago, lingers as I write these words. So many of us who lived this history were there. Many have passed on. We will never meet again this way. But our words, thoughts, and actions ripple through the world, and, more intimately, through our own minds, shaping and changing us. These facts go far beyond love, like, dislike, or any feelings we may have. The way we know the world depends on those come and gone before us. The challenge left us is to accomplish all we once wished and wish still for this sorrowful, miraculous world. Memory gives difficult birth to responsibility.

THE STICKINESS OF PRIVILEGE
AND THE SWAMP OF RACISM

When I visited Mark Rudd and his wife Marla Painter in Albuquerque, he impulsively asked me to say a few words at an upcoming reading of his new book *Underground: My Life in SDS and the Weathermen*. And I impulsively agreed to do so. Mark and I have known each other since coming to Columbia College in 1965. I was in the Columbia strike, a member of the Low Library commune from nearly the beginning to the very end. I've got a small but noticeable protuberance on the right side of my head, an artifact of police violence in the Low bust.

Mark and I (and his partner Sue) became close friends later, during his years in hiding. By strange happenstance, in the mid-70s I was in the Weather Underground while he was out of the organization. Back in the day we talked and argued and broke bread together in places near and far until Mark surfaced in the late 70s.

I was teaching Zen in Santa Fe this March, and when I was done Mark spirited me away to his homestead outside Albuquerque, first pausing for a green chile burrito. Next day we cruised the city in Mark's shabby '92 Chrysler LeBaron, top down on a warm and dusty late winter day. It was an amazing trip, with Mark leaning back in his bucket seat, slouching to the right (this is not a political metaphor), pointing out the architectural highlights of downtown, stopping for fiery and wonderful cholesterol-laden New Mexican food. Everywhere we went, walking the streets, lingering on street-corners, Mark stopped to engage with friends from every walk of life. This, I guess, is what an aging organizer does. I was happy to be along for the ride.

We got into conversation about our kids — each of us has a daughter and son, Mark's kids a bit older than mine. Our children are prospering, well-balanced, ambitious, and blessed by good education. Reflecting on our children's actual and potential success, I was taken with a particular notion — the stickiness of privilege.

Despite concerted efforts to de-class myself — the Columbia occupation, Weather politics, peace and solidarity work, marginal income, years of wandering through an existential wilderness, fortunately arriving at Zen Buddhism — privilege was and is still available to me. Realities of Ivy League education, upper-middle-class Jewish roots, and social connections trump our various concerted efforts to drop out, and our vow not to drop back in. When Mark surfaced in 1977 he was able to walk in and out of courthouses without having to post bail, without doing time. This was incredible even to him. I have had no legal problems stemming from past connections, though I do wonder about all those blacked-out passages in my Freedom of Information documents.

Our children seem easily to inherit this privilege. At home in Berkeley, Laurie and I joke that one day some years ago our daughter Silvie took a look around and decided she'd rather not be downwardly mobile like her parents.

Contrast the stickiness of privilege with the legacy of racism that haunts a group of aging Black activists and community organizers charged as the San Francisco 8. These men, tested and respected in their communities, now face revived charges stemming from the 1971 killing of a San Francisco police officer. In 1975, the court dismissed these charges citing legal misconduct and the torture of witnesses and defendants.

Thirty-five years later, these Black men faced murder and conspiracy charges all over again.

Contrast it with the case of the African-American Harvard scholar Henry Louis Gates, accused of breaking into his own home, then arrested for being angry about it. Here is a guy who lives high in the ivory tower, but, in the eyes of the Cambridge police, just another suspicious black man. So oppression, too, has this sticky quality. Someone said the other day: yeah, shit is sticky, too.

We can't easily shake this weird thing — privilege. Without getting into an extended Buddhist analysis, it is like karma, the subtle interplay of cause and effect — race, class, education, and so on. In fact, I'd say this is karma. Whether we choose to accept it or not, it is inescapable and must be reckoned with.

I recall what the Buddha wrote in the *Dhammapada*:

> I do not call a person a brahmin merely by reason of birth,
> Or if he was born of a noble mother.
> Only if free of all attachments, from worldly grasping,
> Then do I call him a brahmin.

> Whoever is not afraid of breaking their chains,
> Whoever has escaped from ties of attachment,
> That person I call a brahmin.

I am not discounting Mark's sincere work and the relentless honesty of his self-questioning book. If anything, I am appreciating it. I am not discounting my own work and the efforts of so many of us. We cannot shake this privilege thing that sticks to us like sidewalk chewing gum on a rubber-soled shoe. But I hope can we keep trying to use it wisely for the benefit of others. At this late date can we conjure up respect for each other rather than carp about the past, bemoaning and hiding our shortcomings?

This brings to mind a favorite Bob Dylan lyric. His words seem to give voice to a debate the singer is having with himself.

> Now each of us has his own special gift
> And you know this was meant to be true
> If you don't underestimate me,
> I won't underestimate you.

Recognizing these gifts, we reach beyond the narrow places of our background and history. If a gift is to have life and worth, it must always remain in motion. So pass it on, please.

BUDDHAS BEHIND RAZOR WIRE: PRACTICING WITH THE WOMEN OF FCI-DUBLIN

Socially engaged Buddhism takes a variety of forms here in the west. What I mean by engaged Buddhism is really not different from Shakyamuni's basic teachings. He said: "I teach about suffering and the end of suffering." But in this age of globalization and the exploitation of interdependence, socially engaged Buddhism widens the view of suffering and liberation, beyond the focus on an individual or a small sangha/practice community, to social systems and structures. These systems — cities, nations, races, men, women, ecological regions, and so on — are of course made up of individuals. But each "individual" in Buddhist terms is him or herself an impermanent collection of causes and conditions. Humans habitually think an individual ("I, me, mine") exists within one particular bag of skin. The wider and deeper view is that we actually co-construct reality and identity. Taking a leap, I might say that the individual is created by the systems and interactions of all the infinite selves that constitute a system.

The practice of engaged Buddhism entails insight and action exactly where self and social structures come together, moving freely between them as appropriate. This effort — manifesting in areas of social change and protest, social service, environmental activism, hospice work, justice and democracy, civil rights, and more — is beyond charity or well-intentioned service. It has the potential to transform self and others alike.

What follows is my experience and understanding in one realm of engagement.

* * *

I've been driving out to FCI-Dublin — a Federal women's prison and prison camp thirty miles from Berkeley — at least monthly for the last dozen years. Finding a spot in the parking lot, I take a few minutes to collect myself, reflecting that anything can happen when I walk through the gates. I'm not talking about overt violence by inmates or personal danger. These are remote possibilities. Rather, that the facility could be locked down and I will simply have to turn around and go home, or there'll be no one in the chaplain's office to escort me, my paperwork has been lost, a gate officer will be rude, officious, or difficult. These things all happen from time to time. So I sit in the car and remember I am there for the women and for the dharma. I find a smile and walk to the gatehouse.

The meditation group at FCI-Dublin was established by my dharma sister Maylie Scott in affiliation with Buddhist Peace Fellowship when Maylie was visiting imprisoned anti-nuclear activists in the 90s. I took a regular teaching slot in 1998, and soon after became the program's coordinator, gathering a team of teachers with backgrounds in several different Buddhist traditions. All these years we have had the fortunate supervision of Protestant Chaplain Hans Hoch, who has been a true support and a good friend.

The program began as "meditation and stress reduction," initially seen as part of the prison's medical and psychological resources. It evolved into a religious service. By the time I joined, the weekly teachers were all Buddhists. We are not exactly teaching Zen or Vipassana or any particular brand or school of Buddhism. Basically, we are offering meditation and associated activities as tools for an awakened life. I am open about my Zen Buddhist background as the source of the teachings I have to share, but since the group is diverse and self-selected — Catholics, Protestants, Jews, Muslims, as well as Buddhists — we are more accurately presenting Buddhism with a small "b," no proselytizing. I see this as a kind of inter-faith ministry.

FCI-Dublin is one of just a few federal centers for immigration violations, so many of the prisoners are Hispanic. (We usually count on the women to translate for each other.) The inmates include a few women with previous meditation experience, and several have a strong yoga practice. Many practice daily in their cells. While my emphasis has always been on zazen, each teacher has his or her own approach. One of our teachers is a skilled *qigong* instructor, so he regularly shares this practice with the inmates. Another, a professional writer, does an in-the-moment writing practice. Each of us works from our respective tradition. By agreement we do not present one single methodology or practice, but from time to time the teachers meet to check in about how things are going, and to agree on a general direction of study and inquiry.

Bowing and chanting is optional — not all the women are comfortable with elements of Buddhist liturgy. Some see meditation as prayer. But most are curious about Buddhism, and like having some ritual. Over the years, when there has been illness or death affecting someone in the group, we have done simple well-being and memorial ceremonies. On my days at the prison we offer incense and do three full bows towards the altar, then three bows to each other, facing into the circle. I demonstrate how to bow and explain that we are bowing to the Buddha not as an external deity but as a way of honoring the reality of our own true nature. We chant my sister Maylie Scott's *metta* prayer simultaneously in English and Spanish.

May I be well, loving, and peaceful.
May all beings be well, loving, and peaceful.

May I be at ease in my body, feeling the ground beneath my
seat and feet, letting my back be long and straight,
enjoying breath as it rises and falls and rises.
May I know and be intimate with body mind,
whatever its feeling or mood, calm or agitated,
tired or energetic, irritated or friendly.
Breathing in and out, in and out, aware, moment by moment,
of the risings and passings.
May I be attentive and gentle towards my own discomfort
and suffering.
May I be attentive and grateful for my own joy and well-being.
May I move towards others freely and with openness.
May I receive others with sympathy and understanding.
May I move towards the suffering of others
with peaceful and attentive confidence.
May I recall the Bodhisattva of compassion;
her 1,000 hands, her instant readiness for action,
each hand with an eye in it, the instinctive knowing what to do.
May I continually cultivate the ground of peace for myself
and others and persist, mindful and dedicated to this
work, independent of results.
May I know that my peace and the world's peace are not
separate; that our peace in the world is a result of our
work for justice.
May all beings be well, happy, and peaceful.

Meditation goes for about a half hour, starting with five or ten
minutes of basic instruction on sitting and mindfulness. In the
prison atmosphere of social control, I tend to be loose about
the form of meditation, not emphasizing formal posture as I
might at Berkeley Zen Center. There is enough formality and
external control in these women's lives. The important thing
here is for prisoners to feel safe "outside," to have a chance to
sit quietly and meet themselves. This in itself is a rare and precious thing in prison. (As natural as it is, this kind of gathering,
sangha, is rare in the wider world as well.) After meditation I

take time for questions and check-in, or a brief teaching. Over time, we have studied the Four Noble Truths, precepts, the five hindrances, and other points of basic Buddhism. But our discussions always proceed from the women's experience and from the wisdom of their root cultures and religions.

We don't really need a special place to practice. It is wonderful to be able to come to a dedicated meditation hall, but I find that one can meditate anywhere — in a temple, in a railway station, in a prison. Silence is deep in the chapel. Meanwhile people walk by, talking in the hall. A work crew sets up near our windows. Birds sing freely in the trees, and then you hear the chatter of gunfire from the nearby pistol range. All of this is part of one's moment-by-moment awareness. Again prison is all about social control; there's a surveillance camera in the chapel. Authorities can and do invoke rules at will. The federal system seems to be constantly cutting down prisoners' opportunities and rights. Women live together in large dormitories or "pods" with four people to a room. There is ethnic and racial tension. There is unexpected harmony, too. You can feel it, like a cool breeze.

I find a particular challenge working in prisons, and this is something that often confronts engaged Buddhists. According to one's view, meditation itself may or may not be sufficient. The Buddha taught three great principles — *sila, samadhi*, and *prajna* or ethics/morality, meditation, and wisdom. As dharma these three are inseparable and interdependent. But in our modern world meditation can become a kind of technique, a self-improvement project, de-linked from ethics and wisdom.

My view is probably controversial, but when I hear about mindfulness being used in corporations and even taught to soldiers going into combat, I worry about the larger ethical context. Mindfulness, relaxation, even communication skills can create a process that may appear or even arguably may be ethical within an environment whose purpose is essentially unethical. Historically, Japanese samurai warriors cultivated

Zen, and one can see where that led in the complicity of Buddhist sects with Japan's aggressive and imperialist war in the 20th century. So, when we go to the prisons, are we teaching in a way that encourages a prisoner to examine his or her life and mind in the context of the prison system and society itself? Or are we imparting a technique that offers a kind of spiritual pacification, making it easier for guards and prison authorities to maintain social control? I worry about that.

When I visit FCI-Dublin we come together for meditation. We also study and talk about our lives. There is a lot of trust in the room. A sense of sangha comes from meeting weekly year after year. Along with that trust (and because of it), I feel an obligation to share with the women how I see the U.S. prison system — based on principles of retribution and punishment — as an expression of structural violence and structural suffering unlikely to lead to spiritual and psychological rehabilitation of individual prisoners, or restoration to their victims and society as a whole. My vision of engaged Buddhism is that social service and advocacy necessarily go hand in hand. Offering meditation is the service component; studying the societal basis of our prison system and possible alternative responses to poverty, racism, and crime is what I think of as advocacy.

My objective is not to relieve women of responsibility for the unfolding karma of their particular crimes. (Note that we rarely know anything about a prisoner's conviction or even the length of her sentence, unless such details come out in our discussions.) That is work each prisoner has to do herself, looking closely at her life, and considering how she will choose to live in the future. We have spent many intimate hours at FCI-Dublin talking about this in moving and sometimes disturbing ways. But we also need to investigate broader causes and conditions that lead the U.S. to have the largest single prison population and the highest rate of incarceration in the world, according to the government's own National Institute of

Corrections. With 5% of the world's population, we have 23% of the world's prisoners, more than 2,400,000 behind bars, and many millions more in the parole and probation systems.

It would take volumes to explain why this is so. But in dharma terms people and systems are driven by greed, hatred, and delusion. Greed motivates America's vast hidden prison industries, which employ hundreds of thousands of imprisoned men and women, and the privatization of state prisons, which as corporations are even more distant from accountability than their state counterparts. Anger, hatred, and fear generate draconian measure like "three-strikes" and the barbaric death penalty; it is the basis for a racist criminal justice system that locks up poor black and brown men and women far out of proportion to their numbers in the population. Delusion is the only word I can find that accounts for social logic that argues the way one reduces violence in society is by doing violence to those one fears. When has this ever worked?

Inside the prison I am measured in my words and views. What I have expressed in these sentiments above is certainly not the perspective of the Bureau of Prisons, or what they teach us in the annual re-training sessions. But if the dharma of freedom is about relationship — to oneself, to others, to the world — then I feel obligated to help these women cultivate a wide view. Without such a view, bitterness and despair are likely to arise.

* * *

Inside the prison there are rules, and there are rules. These are carefully explained to all prison staff and volunteers. No touching, no favors, no exchange of personal information, no use of first names, and so on. Prison authorities worry about security. This is the shadow dimension of social control. The more one side is controlled, the more resistance and pushback will arise. The prison is also concerned about the natural sympathy one might have for prisoners, and how prisoners can take advantage of that. As the saying goes: They don't call them "cons" for nothing. If one ignores these rules, sooner or later one's ability to work inside will be compromised.

But the dharma itself offers rules for life, and some of these seem to conflict with the rigidity of institutional thinking. Treating all life as part of oneself implies a manner that is close and respectful. So within the confines of our meditation group we are on a first-name basis. I agree it's inappropriate for me to touch the women, so I can't adjust posture as I might in the *zendo*. According to regulations hugs are out of bounds, but from time to time one-armed hugs happen spontaneously. A natural and respectful intimacy is essential.

We have a steady and growing group of 20 to 25 women sitting together. Several have been with us from the beginning. One political prisoner has an 80-year sentence. Over time I have seen many women change, settle into their lives, put aside reactivity, and acknowledge their difficulties, shortcomings, and past harmful actions. This is a wonderful thing to witness, testimony to the ever-present possibility of change that is obvious to me, Chaplain Hoch, and the women themselves. It encourages us to keep our practice going.

I love to see how people live out their beliefs. At FCI-Dublin, I witness how deep people's faith goes. I see women who have committed crimes and made serious mistakes, who are far from home and family, yet have a clear sense that there's something larger than themselves beyond the prison walls. They may be justly or unjustly convicted, but they learn that they can make use of their months and years in prison. Old Zen master Joshu told his disciple, "You are used by the twenty-four hours; I use the twenty-four hours." Even behind bars one can learn to use the twenty-four hours.

No one wants to be in prison. (And my sense is that many of these women should not be in prison. They got tangled up in someone's bad drug deal, or implicated in a boyfriend's illegal activity.) But once inside, one can either make it an opportunity or nurture bitterness. I'm lucky to spend time with the women who want to work, whose way-seeking mind leads them to meditate and study. So each time we sit down together, behind the fences and walls, with guards and countless rules, bad food and long days — even with all that to contend with, liberation is rising.

WORDS SPOKEN ON THE EVE OF STEPHEN ANDERSON'S EXECUTION

Brothers and sisters. How many more times must we bear witness at San Quentin's gates on the eve of an execution? Very soon now, the state of California will take the life of Stephen Wayne Anderson for the confessed murder of Elizabeth Lyman nearly twenty-two years ago.

At this moment our breath mingles with his breath and with each other's breath. We breathe in and come to life. We breathe out, and gently, sorrowfully, let go of life. Please let us take some breaths in silence together.

Bearing witness, we are present with all life. Bearing witness we remember, we call to mind many beings. We call to mind Stephen Anderson, whose remaining time is so short. We call to mind Elizabeth Lyman, whose life was so chillingly taken all those years ago. We remember her family, who continue to grieve her. We call to mind the late Donald Ames, Stephen Anderson's attorney. With compassion we call to mind Governor Davis and Warden Woodford. We call to mind the officers whose difficult task is to lead a prisoner down that last path and administer the lethal infusion.

We remember all the six hundred men and women living year after year on the death row here at San Quentin and at

Chowchilla. We remember all the victims and all those left behind who still grieve.

Bearing witness, we acknowledge the complete interbeing of all life. All living beings breathe as we are breathing. And every molecule of air that was ever breathed continues to circulate. In each of us, warm blood flows as a river. This is true whether we are thoroughly enlightened or deeply deluded. This truth is sacred and ordinary. The Buddha's words tell us that: "All tremble before the rod of punishment; life is dear to each of us; likening others to oneself, one should neither kill nor cause others to kill."

We bear witness to each other, and with each other. Each person out here at the gates right now is fully a part of this moment, irrespective of political views, states of mind, position or uniform. We are out here because Stephen Anderson is up there in those buildings preparing to die. It may not be his intention, but this is Stephen Anderson's offering, the opportunity for us to be in peace together.

If we are to see this as an offering, our responsibility is to keep this gift in motion, to keep it alive. We can move beyond the witness of this cold night to a vow of compassionate action. There is a campaign in California for a death penalty moratorium. Each of us here tonight can join in this effort, honoring the principle of justice and breaking the cycle of state violence. Please remember this as you walk away tonight. If each of us takes up this vow tonight to work for a moratorium — and it will be long, hard work — then we can take heart in our presence right now. And we can embody the peace we wish for Stephen Anderson and Elizabeth Lyman and for thousands more caught up in violence and dread who make their journeys beyond this life.

— *San Quentin Prison, 28 January 2002*

JUKAI AT SAN QUENTIN

The Dharma is a persistent blossom. Even in the brick-stone-steel world of San Quentin, it flowers through cracks in the concrete. On a warm Sunday evening in late February, five men from San Quentin's Buddhadharma Sangha received the precepts, what we call lay ordination, from Seido Lee DeBarros and Myogen Steve Stucky, Zen priests in the San Francisco Zen Center family. Diana Lion and I from Buddhist Peace Fellowship were privileged to witness this turning of the wheel.

At twilight twenty prisoners came across the chapel courtyard. As the sun faded, small black birds settled in a small palm tree, singing loudly. We all entered the chapel and set up a floating zendo for the evening, as these men have been doing weekly for two and a half years.

The zendo itself is a low rectangular room, maybe twenty feet by forty. With fluorescent lights, worn linoleum, and celotex ceiling tiles, it conveys a dingy 1950s aura, nothing holy at all. There are two doors to this space with a handpainted sign over each door. One sign reads "Community of Al-Islam," the other "Congregation Beth Shalom." The men set up orderly rows of cushions, with nice, thick zabuton that they made themselves. They roll out an elegantly crafted altar also made by prisoners. So this shabby space is a refuge for three faiths.

The irony of scarce prison resources is that within institutional limitations a rare reality arises: three religious traditions sharing a common place of worship.

On Sunday evenings the men sit zazen together, do walking meditation, hear and discuss the dharma in a way that offers freedom even in the midst of captivity. The group is diverse: Anglo, Asian, Black, Latino. They tend to be of middle age, because these are men with long sentences who are part of the steady San Quentin population. Another section of the prison is peopled by younger men who are there for classification before transferring to other prisons around the state. There is also the largest death row in the United States, and an "adjustment center" holding several hundred men in solitary confinement.

Tonight six men led by an attendant from Green Gulch Zen Center enter the makeshift zendo chanting in low voices — *Om Namu Shakamuni Butsu*, I take refuge in Shakyamuni Buddha. The Buddhadharma Sangha offers a space of silence and safety within San Quentin. These men have been mainstays in the sangha. It would not have happened without them. They bowed and took places kneeling — six solid-looking men, graying hair, mustaches, wearing freshly laundered prison "blues." The ceremony was an ordination that might have happened anywhere, a ritual of taking refuge in buddha, dharma, sangha, and receiving the sixteen Bodhisattva precepts. Each ordinee also received a lineage document with a Buddhist name. The names created by Seido and Myogen, each consisting of four Sino-Japanese characters, express some personal quality they saw in the man before them. Names like *Seigen Joshi* — Vow Manifesting/Silent Lion, *Jinryu Eishu* — Benevolent Dragon/ Endless Effort, and *Shingyu Fudo* — Faithful Buffalo/Universal Path sound better in Japanese, I think. But in any language they convey strength of character and aspiration to practice.

This is not what we usually expect from longtime prisoners. Each of these men had been in inside for nearly twenty years, convicted of violent crimes. Five of the six had been

Vietnam veterans. They had done harm in their life and were serving hard time for their actions. The karma of violence and the retribution of prison life might have hardened them. Yet as they received their vows, their new name, and a *wagesa* (a ritual garment like a long collar) made by the Green Gulch Sangha, their eyes filled with tears. So did mine. And while solemn and joyful vows were exchanged, a coincidental gospel choir in a chapel across the way sang their hearts out.

Our 13th century Zen ancestor Dogen was filled with a great vow to practice the Buddha's way. Three years ago some of these men in San Quentin wrote to Buddhist Peace Fellowship for help getting a Buddhist practice group going there. It seemed unlikely, but on this night the Dharma not only flowered but bore fruit. Six new bodhisattvas were born in the most unlikely place. It reminds me of ancient encouraging words that Dogen passed to us:

> *Those who in past lives were not enlightened will now be enlightened. In this life, save the body which is the fruit of many lives. Before Buddhas were enlightened, they were the same as we. Enlightened people of today are exactly as those of old... Repenting in this way, one never fails to receive profound help from all Buddhas and Ancestors.*

A DECLARATION OF INTERDEPENDENCE: TRANSFORMING THE THREE POISONS FOR THE SAKE OF ALL SENTIENT BEINGS

— July 2006

As concerned global citizens and as members of a diverse Buddhist community, we want to contemplate and question the role of government in creating a civil and compassionate society. From the standpoint of interconnectedness, those of us living in the United States have a special responsibility to the whole world to explore this question. We know our government is in a position to effect great changes all across this world — change that can be both positive and negative.

Like most people, we are concerned about war in the Middle East, terrorism, the environment, deteriorating public schools, low-paying jobs, racism, and vanishing civil liberties. We are concerned that politics as usual — whether Democratic or Republican —offers little or no meaningful change of direction. Yet we refuse to succumb to apathy, cynicism, or anger. We seek a politics rooted in compassion and generosity born in each of us. Compassion means, literally, to suffer with, to recognize our human connection across all lines of race, culture, nationality, and identity. Generosity means to give freely of what we have, because giving to others is the natural expression of seeing others as ourselves.

Buddhist practice and ethical precepts call forth a range of beneficial views that apply as much to society as to individuals. Twenty-five hundred years ago, when Shakyamuni Buddha was enlightened under the Bodhi Tree, he said, "Now I am awakened together with all sentient beings." Every person on the planet has the full capacity to wake up from the mistaken notion that we are separate from each other. Each of us is connected interdependently with all others, including those who disagree with us. This understanding leads to a reverence for the preciousness of all sentient life.

There are barriers, however, that make people and nations believe that they are separate. From a Buddhist perspective, the "three poisons" of greed, hatred, and delusion cloud our minds and skew our actions:

• *Greed* is the driving force in a consumer society that supports un-democratic corporations that sell us things we don't need. Greed is also at the root of a system in which people, including government officials, are corrupted by the seemingly insatiable appetite for money and power. Looking deeply, we see that nothing can truly be hoarded, accumulated, or held on to. We understand, too, that those things we take from others that are not freely given — resources, labor, wealth, votes, and more — are the birthright of all people. All people have the right to decide how these resources are used.

• *Hatred* gives birth to war, prejudice, and repression. Those forces tend to perpetuate themselves in a ceaseless cycle of violence and militarism. As Buddhism and other faith traditions affirm, "Hatred does not cease by hatred, but only by love." Hatred is rooted in separateness; compassion is rooted in connection. Which way do we wish to turn?

• **Delusion,** or ignorance, stems from our tendency not to see reality just as it is. We are schooled in delusion by systems of indoctrination and mass media that condition us from early childhood to buy into the false promises of consumerism and American exceptionalism. Delusion is the driving force evident in our ever-more centralized media.

And finally, we do not have government of the people, by the people, and for the people. Rather, government has become a holding company for corporate control. When we fail to point out the unraveling of our democratic system, and — as the government's failed response to Hurricane Katrina made clear — the way in which so many citizens lack even the necessities for a self-respecting life, we have fallen prey to the delusion of separateness, and we simultaneously disempower ourselves and others.

The current political and economic system is tainted by these poisons, which necessarily reinforce each other. When we spend many billions of dollars in foreign wars premised on lies and distortions, we have no money to buy food, medicine, and first-class education for the poor at home...or for displaced peoples in need around the world. So a spiral of anger, resentment, need, and confusion spins on and on.

Yet we are called to participate in this very system, even with all its injustices and inequalities. The task before us requires presence of mind, awareness, patience, and perseverance. We wish to be part of a polity that is genuinely representative and fully participatory.

All of us — whatever our faith, political affiliation, cultural background, or economic status — have the same wish for safety and well-being. We may agree or disagree with each other. We may approve or disapprove of a given candidate or representative's positions. But in these decisive times, when so much is at stake, we must act with courage.

Traditional Buddhist teachings invite us to consider the well-being of the generations to come, seeing the future of parents, children, and loved ones. How will our loved ones be impacted if we fail to take care of the present? This kind of care calls for transformation: personal, political, economic, social, and cultural. Transformation is difficult work. We are often afraid to exchange a familiar situation — even one that causes us suffering — for a future that is unknown. Our challenge is to step into the unknown and not fear change or discomfort. Our challenge is to understand that principled conflict is often the midwife of transformation.

With these principles in mind, we offer three areas of transformation to apply when designing policies that will shape lives around the world. As students of the Buddha's way of wisdom and compassion, we vow to practice these principles in our own lives, and to bring this understanding into our work in the social and political realms:

- **Transform greed into generosity.**

- **Transform hatred into love and compassion.**

- **Transform ignorance into clarity and attention.**

The Declaration of Independence of the United States says, "All men [and women] are created equal." In Buddhism, the corollary teaching is that within each of us there is innate goodness and wholeness. Actualization of these ideals is only possible in a life-affirming society. Therefore, it is our responsibility to create the social conditions and political structures that enable people to live with dignity, honor, safety, and sufficient resources.

Only by working together can we renew our world. Only by working together can we insure that the U.S. will fulfill its promise of liberty and justice for all. In our hearts we long to see this vision born anew. As engaged Buddhists and spiritual activists, we commit ourselves to this path.

QUESTIONS FOR REFLECTION AND DISCUSSION

1. How do the three poisons of greed, hatred, and delusion manifest in my own life as a global citizen? For example, what are my consumption patterns around food, oil, and other limited resources?

2. What is one way in which I can work to transform my personal relationship to greed, hatred, or delusion? How can my dharma practice support this process of transformation?

3. How do the three poisons manifest in the social and political structures in my local region? For example, how does ignorance take form in our school/educational system?

4. What is one local issue that I would like to engage with, and what are some ways that I can support the cultivation of generosity, compassion, and clarity in this area?

SOJUN MEL WEITSMAN: BERKELEY ZEN CENTER — 2006

THINGS FALL APART — AN APPRECIATION OF MY TEACHER, SOJUN MEL WEITSMAN

I sit at the computer this morning considering teachings I have received from Sojun Roshi over many years — teachings I understand, half-understand, or don't understand yet. The 2008 election is rapidly approaching and the world economy is in free-fall. Financial institutions are crumbling. Jobs and retirement funds are disappearing. I worry about how to pay the bills, how this will impact my daughter at college on the East Coast, how poor people in projects down the block will make it at all. Like millions around the globe I wonder what is going to happen. Long ago, in a chilly morning *dokusan*, Sojun gave me a pointedly relevant teaching: let things fall apart.

This teaching, of course, has another side. When things fall apart, other things come together. This is the dharma, the law. Aligning with the dharma, pleasant or unpleasant, is the point of practice. If I look at what Sojun said to me twenty-five years ago and why he said it, I may see how his teaching can help in this time of falling apart. I may also glimpse what is simultaneously coming together.

In the mid 1980s, I had been practicing steadily at Berkeley Zen Center for a year or two. Life was still unsettled in my mid-thirties, but after a decade wandering in the existential wilderness I had found a home at BZC. Having a Zen teacher was a new experience. It was nothing like what I had read or imagined. Sojun was disarmingly warm (despite the heat he could convey with a backward glance or the insistent tapping of a foot if you dragged the *mokugyo* beat during service). Some Zen teachers keep students on a short leash. But Sojun's style was to encourage and watch, in accord with Suzuki Roshi's advice in *Zen Mind, Beginner's Mind*: "To give your sheep or cow a large, spacious meadow is the way to control him. So it is with people; first let them do what they want, and watch them. This is the best policy."

I was surprised to see that I loved the Zen forms and found an affinity for them. Previous religious training suggested otherwise. Five years at the orthodox Great Neck Synagogue had not kindled even a spark of devotion. Hebrew lessons were dry as dust, and our dysfunctional, chaotic, and highly secular home included no Jewish religious practice at all. I was sent to synagogue in deference to my devout maternal grandfather (with whom I was not particularly close). *Bar mitzvah* in 1960 came close on the heels of my parents' difficult divorce. The pain of both these events blurs in memory. After that empty milestone I never went back to Great Neck Synagogue. Twenty-five years passed before I took part in another Jewish ritual.

So, again, I was surprised to see how much feeling I had for walking, bowing, chanting, the intricacies of ceremonies, including the ceremony of zazen itself. Before this I had disdained what I felt to be the falseness of ritual. But I watched Sojun carefully and saw his naturalness. He was very much in his body — I was not. There was nothing inflated or egocentric in the way he moved in the world. His actions seemed mindful. In and out of the zendo, he seemed to walk right down the middle way — not casual or off-hand, never stiff, but flexible.

From my first encounter with Zen — reading Chinese and Japanese poetry in high school and college — it was precisely this "everyday" quality of perception and language that called to me. I remember finding it in each page of Basho's *Narrow Road to the Deep North*, where, late in life, the great Zen poet made a long pilgrimage, documented in narrative and verse. In rare, quiet moments I could sense a luminous quality in life, however ordinary. I understand now that this light — call it "buddhanature" — is always present. It is the vast field of interdependent reality. But sensing this and *realizing* it are not exactly the same. When I read *Zen Mind, Beginner's Mind*, it seemed (and still seems) that Suzuki Roshi understood "things as it is" in just this way. I sensed that Sojun's understanding was much the same. It was natural to want to be like him...or to try to be like I thought he was.

From years as a performing musician I was a quick study. I could see how things in the zendo worked together, the flow of time and space. Along with inspiration from Sojun, I learned from other well-seasoned Zen students there — Maylie Scott, Fran Tribe, Ron Nestor, Diane Rizzetto, Bill Milligan, Raul Moncayo, and others. We had no priests besides Sojun at BZC then, but I modeled myself on these maturing students. Ron and Fran taught me how to ring bells, chant, serve meals, and maintain the formal container of Zen.

But some ungainly creature seemed to arise from the depths of my personality. It must have been lurking there, waiting for certain circumstances to give it life. This creature was perfectionistic, judgmental, bossy, impatient, and highly verbal. He thought he was smarter than others, and therefore suffered. (These tendencies of mine are still at play, alas, though I hope I manage them better.)

As I learned the various zendo positions, I was critical of how other people did their jobs. I found myself getting into others' business. In a sense, this was simply mistrust manifest, unconsciously thinking I could do things better. On a psychological level, I feared that if I did not somehow "fix" the situation at hand, I would be thrown into the void, somehow abandoned. As a child I had a recurring dream: clinging to a speeding car or train, flung into space as it rounded a turn.

Each time the dream occurred, I awoke with a start, never landing.

From time to time, people let me know that this bossy tendency of mine pissed them off. I can't blame them. But after a while I found myself training others. In a training situation — working with someone face-to-face — I was more patient and appreciative. Even though the practice is particular and demanding here at BZC, everyone comes to the zendo with lives that are already very full. They're not monks training at a monastery. We were parents, workers, professionals, people with chronic illness, sitting side by side every morning and afternoon. Sojun emphasized lay practice, but I still didn't get it. I didn't see that everyone at BZC was a volunteer, doing the best he or she could do to sustain Suzuki Roshi's Zen.

Meanwhile, Sojun just let me roam and ruminate. He watched patiently. I like this metaphor of a cow in a large pasture, but BZC often felt very small. Sometimes I felt more like a bull in a china shop. I told people what they should be doing; they got their feelings hurt or became irritated with me, and I could not see what the problem was. All I was doing, I thought, was keeping things together and making the Zen center work.

Sojun watched without reacting. For a long time he sat unmoving, like a frog, watching me. And then, one day, he pounced, swallowing me whole with these words: <u>let things fall apart</u>. This is a bottomless teaching, and I will be grateful for it always. These words will linger to my dying day.

But the meaning is subtle.

Each of us has to decide when to let things fall apart and when to work as hard as one can to insure survival, to allow for new things to arise. That is the koan of political work and social action, which I have been involved in since high school. (Now I call it engaged Buddhism.) Letting things fall apart too easily leans toward resignation and laziness. That's not what Sojun had in mind. And trying to hold on to the present moment or circumstances is simply impossible. Nobody hands out an instruction book. Actually this teaching of Sojun's was given to me as medicine, to bring me into balance. He might tell another person in another circumstance: hold on!

I once asked Sojun about a saying I had heard (which, later, I found came from the Scottish novelist John Buchan): "It's a great life if you don't weaken." He laughed. "Everyone knows that. You never heard this expression before?" It seems to capture something essential about his teaching. If one has a serious disease, one does one's best to get the right medicine and heal properly. If that illness is untreatable, one lives as well as one can, turning towards life and towards those around us for as long as possible. When dying is at hand, falling apart, one turns wholeheartedly to the business of dying. This was Sojun's message to my dharma sister Maylie Scott in her last days. In that case, one might say: "It's a great life even if you do weaken." The point is to be steady and confident, meeting each circumstance as it arises, instead of being pushed around by circumstances.

An old BZC student once described Sojun as lowering his head and diligently pushing on. Another old student described him as "a teddy bear with teeth." That's pretty good! I would be glad to have even twenty percent of Sojun's determination and quiet fierceness. Alas, I am more excitable than that. But from long years working with him, there is a mysterious stability even within my emotionality. This, I think, is faith. Suzuki Roshi said, "The most important point is to accept yourself and stand on your two feet." Beneath our different personalities, backgrounds, and style, this is the essence I have drawn from Sojun's lessons: simply let go and be myself, moment by moment. Fall apart and come together. Come together and fall apart.

APPENDIX 1

THE 28ᵀᴴ CHAPTER OF SHOBOGENZO: BODAISATTA-SHISHOBO THE BODHISATTVA'S FOUR EMBRACING DHARMAS

— **Translated by Shohaku Okumura & Hozan Alan Senauke**

First is giving. Second is loving-speech. Third is beneficial-action. Fourth is identity-action.

GIVING

Giving means to be not greedy. Not to be greedy means not to crave. Not to crave means, in worldly expression, not to flatter. Even if we rule the four continents, in order to offer the teachings of the true Way, we must simply and unfailingly not be greedy. It is like offering treasures that are going to be discarded to people we do not know. Give flowers blooming on the distant mountains to the Tathagata. Offer treasures accumulated in our past lives to living beings. Whether a gift is dharma or material objects, each gift is truly endowed with the virtue of offering. There is a principle that even if a gift is not our personal possession, nothing hinders our practice of offering. A gift is never disregarded for its small value — but our effort should be genuine.

When the Way is entrusted to the Way, we attain the Way. When we attain the Way, the Way unfailingly continues to be entrusted to the Way. When treasures are entrusted to treasures, these treasures certainly become giving. We offer ourselves to ourselves, and we offer others to others. The causal relation of giving has a power that pervades the heavens above and the human world below. It even reaches the realm of the wise and holy who have attained the fruits of realization. This is because, in becoming a giver or a receiver, we establish an affinity with all beings in the entire world.

The Buddha said, "When a person who practices offering comes into an assembly, other people watch that person with admiration."

We should know that the mind of such a person is imperceptible and everywhere. Therefore if we should offer even a single word or a single verse of dharma, it will become a seed of goodness in this lifetime and in other lives to come. We should give even humble things such as a single penny or a single stalk of grass. They will spread roots of goodness in this age and other ages. Dharma can be a material treasure, and a material treasure can be dharma. This depends upon the giver's vow and wish.

Indeed, by offering a beard, a Chinese emperor harmonized his retainer's mind, and by offering sand, a child gained a throne. Such people did not covet rewards from others; they just shared what they had according to their ability. To launch a boat or build a bridge is the practice of *dana-paramita*. When we carefully study the meaning of giving, both receiving our body and giving up our body are offering. Earning a livelihood and managing a business are, from the outset, nothing other than giving. Entrusting flowers to the wind, and entrusting birds to the season may also be the meritorious action of giving. Both givers and receivers should thoroughly grasp the principle that Great King Ashoka's offering of half a mango to hundreds of monks was a vast and boundless offering. We should not only cultivate our body's power to make offerings, but we should be careful not to overlook any suitable opportunities. From the beginning, because we are truly endowed with the virtue of giving, we have received our present lives.

The Buddha said, "A gift may even be received and used by oneself; moreover one can pass it to one's parents, wife, and children." Therefore we should see that using gifts ourselves is a kind of offering, and to give to our parents, wife, and children is also offering. When we can give up even one speck of dust as the practice of giving, though it is a small act, we can quietly rejoice in it. This is because we have already correctly transmitted and carried out one of the virtues of the buddhas, and because we have practiced a bodhisattva's act for the first time.

The mind of a sentient being is hard to change. We begin to transform the mind ground of sentient beings by offering material things, so we resolve to continue to transform them until they all attain the Way. From the beginning we should always practice offering. This is why the first of the six *paramitas* is *dana-paramita*. A wide or narrow mind cannot be measured; the greatness or smallness of material things cannot be weighed. But there are times when our mind turns things, and there is giving, in which things turn our mind.

LOVING-SPEECH
Loving-speech means whenever meeting sentient beings, first arouse compassionate mind toward them, and offer caring and loving words. In general, we should not use violent or harmful words. In society, there is a tradition of asking others

if they are well. In the buddha way we have the words "Take good care of yourself!" and the disciple's filial duty to ask their teachers, "How are you?" It is loving-speech to speak with the intention of "compassionately caring for living beings as if they were our own babies."

We should praise those with virtue and pity those without virtue. From the moment we begin to delight in loving-speech, it grows little by little. When we practice this way, loving-speech, which is usually invisible and unknown, will manifest itself. In our present bodily life, we should unfailingly be willing to practice loving-speech, and continue through many ages and lives.

Whether we are subduing a deadly foe or making peace among people, loving-speech is fundamental. When one hears loving-speech that person's face becomes happy and their mind becomes joyful. When one hears of someone else's loving-speech, that person inscribes it in their heart and soul. We should know that loving-speech arises from a loving mind, (*shin* or heart/mind) and the seed of a loving mind is a compassionate heart. Study the way that loving-speech has the power to transform the world. It is not merely praising someone's abilities.

BENEFICIAL-ACTION

Beneficial-action means to create skillful means to benefit all living beings whether they are noble or humble. For example, we care for the near and far futures of others, and carry out skillful means to benefit them. We should pity a cornered tortoise and take care of a sick sparrow. When we see a lost tortoise or a sick sparrow, we help them without expecting any reward, motivated solely by beneficial-action itself.

An ignorant person may think that if we focus on the benefit of others, our own benefit will be excluded. This is not the case. Beneficial-action is all of the dharma; it extensively benefits both self and others. There was man in ancient times who tied up his hair three times while he took a bath, and stopped eating three times while he had one meal. He only had a mind to benefit others. He never withheld instructions to people of other countries.

Therefore, we should equally benefit friends and foes; we should benefit self and others alike. Because beneficial actions never regress, if we attain this mind, we can perform beneficial-action even for grass, trees, wind, and water. We should just strive to help the ignorant beings.

IDENTITY-ACTION

Identity-action means not to be different — neither different from self nor from others.

For example, it is like the way that the Tathagata identifies himself with human beings in the human world. Because he identifies himself in the human world, we know that he does the same in other worlds. When we know identity-action, self and others are one suchness. Harps, poems, and wine make friends with human beings, make friends with heavenly beings, and make friends with spirits.

Human beings make friends with harps, poems, and wine. There is a principle that harps, poems, and wine make friends with harps, poems, and wine; that human beings make friends with human beings; that heavenly beings make friends with heavenly beings, and that spirits make friends with spirits. This is how we study identity-action.

For example, "action" means form, dignity and attitude. After letting others identify with our "self," there is the principle of letting our "self" identify with others. Relations between self and others vary infinitely depending on time and conditions.

Guanzi says, "The ocean does not refuse water; therefore it is able to achieve its vastness. Mountains do not refuse the earth, therefore they are able to become lofty. Wise rulers do not weary of people, therefore they have a large number of followers."

We should know that, for the ocean, not to refuse water is identity-action. We should further know that the virtue of water that does not refuse the ocean is also fulfilled. This is the reason why water is able to come together to form the ocean, and earth is able to pile up to form mountains. We should know intimately that because the ocean does not refuse to be the ocean, it can be the ocean and achieve greatness; because mountains do not refuse to be mountains they can be mountains and achieve loftiness.

Because wise rulers do not weary of their people they attract a large number of people. "A large number of people" means a nation. "A wise ruler" may mean an emperor. Emperors do not weary of their people. They do not weary of their people, but this does not mean that they fail to give rewards and punishments. Even though they mete out necessary rewards and punishments, they have no hatred toward the people. In ancient times, when people were gentle and honest, there were no rewards and punishments in the country. The rewards and punishments of those days were different from those of today.

Even these days, there must be some people who seek the Way with no expectation of reward. This is beyond the thought of ignorant people. Because wise rulers are brilliant, they do not weary of their people. Although people unfailingly have the desire to form a nation and to find a wise ruler, few of them fully understand the reason why a wise ruler is a wise ruler. They are glad simply to be accepted by the wise ruler. But they never recognize that they themselves do accept and support the wise ruler. Thus the principle of identity-action exists both in the wise ruler and ignorant people. This is why identity-action is the practice and the vow of a bodhisattva. Truly and simply and we should face all beings with a gentle expression.

Because each of these four embracing actions includes all the other four embracing actions, there are sixteen embracing actions.

Written on the 5th day of the 5th lunar month in the 4th year of Ninji (1243) by Monk Dogen who went to Sung China and transmitted the Dharma.

APPENDIX 2

SELECTED BIBLIOGRAPHY

Aitken, Robert. *Mind of Clover: Zen Ethics.* North Point: San Francisco, 1982.

Aitken, Robert. *The Practice of Perfection: The Paramitas from a Zen Buddhist Perspective.* Counterpoint: Berkeley, 1997.

Ambedkar, B.R. *The Buddha and His Dharma.* People's Education Society: Mumbai, 1984.

Aung San Suu Kyi. *Freedom From Fear.* Penguin: New York, 1991.

Baldoquin, Hilda Gutierrez, ed. *Dharma, Color, and Culture: New Voices in Western Buddhism.* Parallax: Berkeley, 2004.

Sister Chan Khong. *Learning True Love: How I Learned to Practice Social Change in Vietnam.* Parallax: Berkeley, 1993.

Eppsteiner, Fred, ed. *The Path of Compassion: Writings on Socially Engaged Buddhism.* Parallax: Berkeley, 1988.

Glassman, Bernie. *Bearing Witness: A Zen Master's Lessons in Making Peace.* Bell Tower: New York, 1998.

Halifax, Joan. *Being with Dying: Cultivating Compassion and Fearlessness in the Presence of Death.* Shambhala: Boston, 2009.

Hyde, Lewis. *The Gift: Imagination and the Erotic Life of Property.* Vintage: New York, 1983.

Jones, Ken. *The New Social Face of Buddhism: A Call to Action.* Wisdom: Somerville, 2003.

Kaza, Stephanie, Kenneth Kraft, eds. *Dharma Rain: Sources of Buddhist Environmentalism.* Shambhala: Boston, 2000.

Kraft, Kenneth. *Inner Peace, World Peace: Essays on Buddhism and Nonviolence.* SUNY, Albany, 1992.

Leighton, Taigen Daniel. *Faces of Compassion: Classic Bodhisattva Archetypes and Their Modern Expression.* Wisdom: Somerville, 2003.

Loy, David. *The Great Awakening: a Buddhist Social Theory.* Wisdom: Somerville, 2003.

Loy, David. *Money Sex War Karma: Notes for a Buddhist Revolution.* Wisdom: Somerville, 2008.

Macy, Joanna. *World As Lover World As Self: Courage for Global Justice and Ecological Renewal.* Parallax: Berkeley, 2007.

Macy, Joanna. *Mutual Causality in Buddhism and General Systems Theory: The Dharma of Natural Systems.* SUNY Press: Albany, 1991.

Maha Ghosananda. *Step By Step: Meditations on Wisdom and Compassion.* Parallax: Berkeley, 1992.

Masters, Jarvis Jay. *Finding Freedom: Writings from Death Row.* Padma: Junction City, 1997.

Masters, Jarvis Jay. *That Bird Has My Wings: The Autobiography of an Innocent Man on Death Row.* Harper One: San Francisco, 2009.

Moon, Susan, ed. *Not Turning Away: The Practice of Engaged Buddhism.* Shambhala: Boston, 2004.

Nhat Hanh, Thich. *Being Peace.* Parallax: Berkeley, 1987.

Nhat Hanh, Thich. *For a Future To Be Possible.* Parallax: Berkeley, 1993.

Omvedt, Gail. *Ambedkar: Towards an Enlightened India.* Penguin: New Delhi, 2004.

Queen, Christopher, Sallie King, ed. *Engaged Buddhism: Buddhist Liberation Movements in Asia.* SUNY: New York, 1996.

Queen, Christopher. *Engaged Buddhism in the West.* Wisdom: Boston, 2000.

Rothberg, Donald. *The Engaged Spiritual Life: A Buddhist Approach to Transforming Ourselves and the World.* Beacon: Boston, 2006.

Sivaraksa, Sulak. *Seeds of Peace: A Buddhist Vision For Renewing Society.* Parallax: Berkeley, 1992.

Stanley, John, David Loy, Gyurme Dorje, eds. *A Buddhist Response to the Climate Emergency.* Wisdom: Somerville, 2009.

Suzuki, Shunryu. *Zen Mind, Beginner's Mind: Informal Talks on Zen Meditation and Practice.* Weatherhill: New York, 1970.

Suzuki, Shunryu. *Not Always So: Practicing the True Spirit of Zen.* Harper Collins: New York, 2002.

Tenzin Gyatso, Dalai Lama XIV. *Ethics for a New Millennium.* Riverhead: New York, 1999.

Victoria, Brian Daizen. *Zen At War.* Weatherhill: New York, 1997.

Watts, Jonathan S., ed. *Rethinking Karma: The Dharma of Social Justice.* Silkworm, Chiang Mai, Thailand, 2009.

APPENDIX 3

BRIEF NOTES ON THE ESSAYS

"To My World" — Back in the day I was entangled in the reading and writing of poetry. This poem poster from the early 70s was illustrated by Nancy Werner. It still seems true.

"The Bodhisattva's Embrace" — Dogen Zenji's "Bodaisatta Shishobo" or "The Bodhisattva's Four Embracing Dharmas" has been a central teaching for me over many years. The text itself is in *Appendix 1*. This essay was published in the journal "Religion East &West."

"Mindfulness Must Be Engaged" — Self-explanatory, previously unpublished.

"Dharma Visions: Sources of Socially Engaged Buddhism" was written by Donald Rothberg & Alan Senauke, adapted for *Turning Wheel* from their presentation at the May 2008 "Path of Engagement" retreat at Spirit Rock Meditation Center.

"What Is To Be Done" — One of several pieces I wrote after the September 11 attack and subsequent U.S. retaliation. This appeared on the BPF website in early 2002.

"Notes Towards a Practical Zen Psychology" — Written in early 2008 after the ideas had been percolating for a long time. My teacher, Sojun Weitsman, brought me to the *Platform Sutra* long ago. And Laurie Senauke was an ever-responsive sounding board.

"Grace Under Pressure" — I wrote this for *Buddhadharma* (Summer 2008), shortly after returning from a witness journey to Rangoon two months after the brutal repression of the Saffron Revolution in the fall of 2008.

"Ambedkar's Children" — Reflections following a remarkable time among Dalit Buddhists in India. Thanks to Mangesh Dahiwale, Dh. Lokamitra, Dh. Maitreyanath, Priyadarshi Telang, Bharat Wankhede, Dh. Vivikamitra, Dh. Viradhamma, and many others who made this journey possible and helped me along the way. I hope to see you all again soon.

"Shipbreaking" — I wrote this from notes and photographs gathered at the shipbreaking yards of Chittagong, Bangladesh in 1999. I can't believe I made this journey, and would love to go back for a longer stay.

"Through a Glass, Darkly: Towards a Buddhist Perspective on Israel & Palestine" was published by *Jewish Voice for Peace* in February of 2004. Comments and critical reading by friends were helpful in the thinking, writing, and rewriting of this piece: Robert Aitken, Kyogen Carlson, Annette Herskovits, Ken Kraft, Wendy Lewis, David Loy, Eve Marko, Susan Moon, Hilton Obenzinger, Santikaro Bhikkhu, Sibylle Scholz, Laurie Senauke, Allan Solomonow, Terry Stein, Jon Watts, and Michael Wenger.

"Walking in the Direction of Beauty: An Interview with Sister Chan Khong" is an interview conducted by Susan Moon and Alan Senauke in 1993. It ran in the Winter 1994 issue of *Turning Wheel*.

"It's the Real Thing" — Sketches of liquid consumption around the world.

"World Faiths Development Dialogue — Reflections One Year Later" — Ah, the last time I saw Rome, 12.99.

"The World Is What You Make It: One Zennist's View of Global Responsibility" — At David Loy's urging, I wrote this for *A Buddhist Response to the Climate Emergency*: Wisdom, 2009.

"On Race & Buddhism" — Written in 1997, later published in *Adbusters*, Jan/Feb 2001.

"What Did You Learn in School Today: Columbia Strike 40 Years Later" — The 1968 uprising and strike at Columbia University is the pivotal point of my formal education. The strike anniversary in April 2008 was another powerful moment. This assembled reflection was included with others on the Strike Anniversary website.

"The Stickiness of Privilege and the Swamp of Racism" — I wrote an earlier version, read at a dialogue between Mark Rudd and Ishmael Reed on the publication of Mark's book *Underground: My Life in SDS and the Weathermen.*

"Buddhas Behind the Razor Wire: Practicing with the Women of FCI-Dublin" was published by *Religion East & West* in 2009.

"On the Eve of Stephen Anderson's Execution" — A cold night in January 2002.

"Jukai at San Quentin" — A moving and amazing ceremony. This short piece ran in *Turning Wheel*.

"A Declaration of Interdependence: Transform the Three Poisons for the Sake of All Sentient Beings" was written in 2004 and presented to delegates of the Republican and Democratic conventions that year. A number of people contributed to drafts, including: Robert Aitken Roshi, Hilda Ryumon Gutiérrez Baldoquín, Maia Duerr, Diane Gregorio, Ken Kraft, Santikaro Larsen, Diana Lion, David Loy, Bob Lyons, Susan Moon, Cliff Reiss, Craig Richards, Donald Rothberg, Cedar Spring, and Diana Winston. The essay was updated in 2006 and guiding questions were added.

"Things Fall Apart" — Sharing an important lesson from Sojun Roshi, my root teacher, which I have been trying to learn for 25 years. It was included in *Umbrella Man — Recollections of Sojun Mel Weitsman by His Dharma Heirs.*

BIOGRAPHY

Hozan Alan Senauke is a Soto Zen Buddhist priest in the tradition of Shunryu Suzuki Roshi. (Hozan, translated as Dharma Mountain, is his Buddhist name.) Alan serves as vice-abbot of Berkeley Zen Center, where he lives with his wife Laurie. They have two children, Silvie and Alexander.

Alan is founder of the Clear View Project, developing Buddhist-based resources for relief and social change. In the last several years, Clear View has supported India's ex-untouchable Buddhists, and Burma's monks, nuns, and activists in their yearning for democracy. He was executive director of Buddhist Peace Fellowship from 1991 through 2001, and remains active in BPF as Senior Advisor. Alan is also a member of the International Network of Engaged Buddhists' Advisory Council.

In another realm, Alan has been a close student and active performer of American traditional music for nearly fifty years.

Clear View Project's website is www.clearviewproject.org.
Alan can be reached at <alan@clearviewproject.org>.

Made in the USA
Middletown, DE
18 April 2021